THE LIFE OF A SPY

ROD BARTON

THE LIFE OF A SPY

ROD BARTON

AN EDUCATION IN TRUTH, LIES AND POWER

Published by Black Inc.,
an imprint of Schwartz Books Pty Ltd
Level 1, 221 Drummond Street
Carlton VIC 3053, Australia
enquiries@blackincbooks.com
www.blackincbooks.com

9781760642778 (paperback)
9781743821763 (ebook)

A catalogue record for this book is available from the National Library of Australia

Cover design by Regine Abos
Text design by Tristan Main
Typesetting by Typography Studio
Cover photograph by Rockfinder / Getty

To Jan,

for persuading me to write this book and for her patience with me during its creation.

CONTENTS

'To live is to choose. But to choose well, you must know who you are and what you stand for, where you want to go and why you want to get there.'

Kofi Annan, Secretary-General of the United Nations 1997–2006

AUTHOR'S NOTE

As our helicopter, piloted by the German Luftwaffe, flew over the western deserts of Iraq, I heard one of the engines splutter and stall. We quickly lost altitude and landed unsteadily on the burning sands. I climbed out and stared across the windswept plain, the heat shimmering to the horizon, and wondered what I was doing here, in the middle of nowhere.

I sat in the shade of the fuselage in the oven-like heat, waiting for the Germans to send a rescue helicopter, reflecting on what an unusual situation I found myself in. I was an intelligence officer with the Australian government, but had moved on from sitting in an office analysing data to participating in an operation I could not have imagined at the start of my career.

And as it turned out, my career only became more remarkable from there.

I was certainly no James Bond with a licence to kill, but I did experience some events that would have intrigued him. I worked with the British intelligence services and with, and for, the CIA. I had guns pointed at me, death threats issued, a price placed on my head. On the less deadly side, I also became an expert in bee excrement and collected Antarctic penguin eggs.

In this book I recount the strange circumstances of my recruitment to the intelligence world and some of the adventures of my professional life. From a naive junior intelligence analyst, through working for Hans Blix as a weapons inspector, to my clashes with the CIA and my wrangle with the politicians who led Australia to war in Iraq in 2003, I have seen a unique side of intelligence operations around the globe, and witnessed things that have both alarmed and reassured me about the capabilities of our intelligence agencies.

This book is not intended as a deep study in the theory and practice of intelligence. It is to inform and, I hope, entertain. Much of the narrative focuses on events in the lead-up to the war in Iraq, and the consequences that followed. I believe there were no winners in the so-called War on Terror, but readers will have to decide this for themselves.

Spies never want to reveal much. For security reasons, there are still some operational details I cannot disclose. Many names have been changed to protect the innocent and, in some cases, the not-quite-so innocent.

Rod Barton
February 2021

CHAPTER 1

GRUNTERS AND GROANERS

'It is a mistake to look too far ahead. Only one link of the chain of destiny can be handled at a time.'

Winston Churchill

On stage at St Philip's Christian College, a private school on the New South Wales central coast, I was tense. I had given many talks and lectures, but this was different. Usually I spoke about the nature of intelligence work or the formulation of United Nations Security Council resolutions, or even weapons of mass destruction and the politics of disarmament. This time, I planned to speak about my work as a weapons inspector in Iraq. Although I didn't want to dumb it down, I couldn't venture far into theory, politics or technicalities. Fifteen- to eighteen-year-olds are a tough audience.

The students had gathered in the assembly hall, some bussed in from nearby schools, so the mob had now grown to more than 200. I might have had more than one gun pointed at me, but now I was nervous in front of a bunch of schoolkids.

As we waited for the last stragglers to take their seats, the principal leaned over and whispered, 'Don't worry if some of the students get up to go to the toilet and don't come back.' Seeing my alarm, she confided, 'This happens when we have guest speakers. It's nothing to do with you.'

I stood at the podium while the principal introduced me and looked at the crowd contemplatively. Most were staring at their phones or chatting. A small group of boys at the back were flicking spitballs at each other. I wondered who would be left in the hall by the end of my talk.

So I broke a long-standing rule and began, slowly and steadily: 'I was a spy for the Australian government.'

Down went the phones. The arcs of spittle-laden projectiles ceased.

Not one student left during the talk. Afterwards, the principal told me that this was a first.

No self-respecting spy would ever out themselves as one. The job is 'intelligence officer', and it comes in different shapes and forms: some collect intelligence from overseas, perhaps through remote electronic surveillance or by running operatives in foreign countries; analysts make sense of what is collected, and assessment officers put this analysis into some sort of context.

Officially, I was an intelligence analyst and an assessment officer, and later a director of intelligence, but when I was posted overseas, the boundaries between collection and analysis became blurred, as did my role in the intelligence world. In that sense, I was a spy.

* * *

My interest in intelligence began early. I was born in the industrial north of England, in a rather bleak post-war Britain, where my father was a research chemist for a soap factory, and my mother a primary-school teacher. They sought a better life for themselves and their four children, so in 1957, when I was nine, they decided to emigrate to sunny South Australia. The choice of destination was influenced by my maternal grandfather, who had run away to sea as a teenager and gave glowing reports of his port of landing in 1896: Glenelg. I knew what a palindrome was due to this family lore. And so we became Ten Pound Poms.

However, palindromes were not in my future. We moved instead to the new migrant town of Elizabeth. It was a rough-and-tumble place with a mix of cultures, as rock star Jimmy Barnes, who also grew up there, detailed in his biography *Working Class Boy*. Most migrants were from the United Kingdom, but there were also sizeable numbers from Germany and the Netherlands. Some of my friends had names like Jürgen and Rudolph, which I considered exotic, and I became interested in key differences between us, such as their speech patterns and what was in their lunchboxes.

Elizabeth was very much a working-class town, especially with the opening of the Holden car factory in 1963. But across the railway tracks there was another large employer: the federal government's Weapons Research Establishment. Some top British and Australian scientists worked on secret projects at WRE. I became curious about what lay behind the double rows of barbed-wire fencing. Occasionally there were exciting clues, such as the roar of static motors, which I later discovered were live-fired in rockets at Woomera, in the state's far north.

Elizabeth South Primary was the only school in this rapidly growing town, and almost 1000 students crowded into its rows of portable classrooms. There was an enthusiastic but stern choirmaster. To audition for his choir, we all had to learn the national anthem. He would pace the long lines of students assembled in the schoolyard, listening to our angelic voices individually. Every so often a child was grabbed by the collar and ousted. And so it was for me: 'Barton, out. Join the grunters and groaners.'

Had I a voice like Jimmy Barnes, no doubt I would never have become a spy. The grunters and groaners – there were about thirty of us – were banished to a classroom to learn geography while the strains of 'The Song of Australia' wafted in through the windows. I didn't mind the extradition, as foreign countries interested me even then. I learnt about faraway places with fascinating names such as Mogadishu, Mombasa and Baghdad. As a wide-eyed ten-year-old, I decided that I would one day visit these places.

The Boy Scouts propelled me further on the path of adventure. On overnight trips, we were taught basic survival skills: cooking on an open fire, reading maps and bush camping. Then, when I was fifteen, the Cuban Missile Crisis entered our world.

The crisis was sparked by the Soviet Union's construction of a base in Cuba, with a plan to equip it with nuclear missiles that could readily strike anywhere in continental America. President Kennedy and Congress declared this intolerable and authorised a blockade of the Soviet ships carrying the missiles to Cuba. The world came close to a nuclear war, but eventually the Russians saw sense and turned the ships around.

Our scouting weekend venture was loosely based on the crisis. Our objective was to find a 'Cuban missile base' hidden somewhere near Adelaide and destroy it. On a cold Friday evening, we were divided into pairs, driven up into the Adelaide Hills and dumped somewhere on the quiet backroads. Sealed instructions revealed that we were to rendezvous the following day, where another car would take us to our next location.

Our second location was the city of Adelaide, where, according to our next set of instructions, we were to proceed to Balfours café on King William Street. At a designated time, we would see a man arrive wearing one pink shoelace. Upon hearing the code phrase 'The roses are in bloom', he would pass us a note with the map coordinates of the hidden missile base. Saturday night was spent back in the Adelaide Hills.

On Sunday we realised that, despite our best efforts in working out the shortest route to the missile base, we had miscalculated. We didn't quite reach the 'electrified fence' in time for the ten-minute window when the power would be cut by resistance fighters. We stood forlornly on the hillside looking down on the fence (rope strung around poles) that protected the missile base and its plywood missile cut-outs. We had failed, but we could see that our fellow adventurers had succeeded. Choking on the taste of disappointment, I vowed to be a better secret agent.

My imagination over spies and special missions had been fired. Although nothing more would come to pass for many years, I was on my way.

* * *

I still harboured ambitions to travel to foreign places, but the next few years were consumed with getting an education. Like my father, I had an interest in science, and I gained degrees in microbiology and biochemistry at the University of Adelaide. But I was still looking for an escape from the confines of Elizabeth.

It came when a recruiter from Canberra visited the university, seeking graduates to join the public service. His mission was not to find members of the secret service but something less illustrious: examiners at the patent office. I knew next to nothing about patents, but I signed on enthusiastically and packed my bags for Canberra.

After nine months of training to qualify as an examiner and a few months of on-the-job experience, I summoned the courage to knock on the Commissioner of Patents' door with a suggestion. Since Australian patent law was based on English law, I suggested, it would be a good idea for me to gain work experience in the British office. The commissioner seemed only half convinced, but nevertheless granted me twelve months' special leave and wrote a letter of recommendation to hand to his counterpart in London.

Three months later, in January 1971, I was on a ship to London, excited by the adventures that lay ahead. Not quite Mogadishu yet, but I could see that this step might eventually lead there.

I managed to spin out my time at the British Patent Office to more than eighteen months, which gave me the opportunity to take trips to Europe from time to time. I was particularly interested to visit East Germany, Poland and the Soviet Union. The world was still in the depths of the Cold War, and these communist countries had been off-limits to Western tourists, but now the doors were opening, albeit slowly. Since I was an Australian public servant working for the British civil service, I had to receive briefings from both governments on the political perils I might face.

For the British briefing, a rather ordinary man, who did not tell me his name or position but I assumed was from MI5, came to my office and asked me to read a short note. This all seemed rather understated and disappointing for my first real contact with the mysterious world of spies.

The Australian briefing was held at Australia House in the Strand, in what, I was to learn later, was the Australian Security Intelligence Organisation (ASIO) office. The experience was more intriguing: I entered a secure cell through doors with special locks. Introductions were first-name only. I doubted that 'Peter' and 'James' were the real names of the men I met anyway.

I was told that on entering the Soviet Union, the little group I was travelling in would be assigned an Intourist guide, a staff member from the primary Soviet travel agency for foreign tourists, but that this guide would really be working for the KGB. I was warned of the possibility of entrapment by attractive Russian women also working for the KGB. This latter was rather good news for a 24-year-old.

Disappointingly, I did not meet any alluring female secret agents on my trip. I did visit the Kremlin for a performance of the Bolshoi Ballet, a particular highlight. It was 4 July 1971, and being at the centre of Soviet power on American Independence Day made it even more memorable. But I knew then that I had to see the other side of the political equation.

On my way home to Australia at the end of my attachment in London, I bought a Greyhound bus ticket and spent six weeks touring the greatest capitalist system the world has ever seen. The contrast with Russia was stark, and although I could see problems in the United States, particularly for the poor, I knew which regime I would rather live under. I was beginning to develop an interest in political systems – a scientist slowly becoming a political scientist.

By the end of 1971, I was back at the patent office in Canberra. Now that I'd had a taste of adventure and travel, the job seemed especially dull, and I was on the lookout for new opportunities. One would appear early the next year, when the Australian government gazette advertised for a junior scientist to perform some vague-sounding duties in the Department of Defence. I decided to apply, even though I couldn't work out what the job actually involved.

On the morning of the interview, I gained some insight. A colleague at the patent office had interviewed for the same position, and he confided some of the questions he was asked. A few were scientific in nature, but most had to do with international politics. 'This is a job where your *intelligence* may come in to play,' he said with a wink.

This gave me some time to prepare my answers. I had no qualms about this: after all, if the job was in intelligence, surely it was a plus if I used all the intel available to me.

I turned up at the Defence headquarters, where I was given a visitor's pass and escorted to a complex marked *Building L*, where another visitor's pass was assigned. A short distance along the ground-floor corridor, my escort stopped outside a large steel door and ushered me inside. As the door closed behind me, I found I was in a windowless vault equipped with a combination lock. This was going to be some interview!

Behind a desk in the centre of the room sat a man in his fifties. I was struck by his tidy dark hair and military bearing. Off to one side sat his secretary, ready to take notes. He introduced himself as Robert Mathams, Director of Scientific and Technical Intelligence. Did I feel comfortable with all the security? Yes, I lied, as any budding intelligence officer would. I had entered a different world, but strangely I felt comfortable.

He said there had been a terrible mistake: when the job descriptions were sent out, I received one that related to another role. He slid a single piece of paper across the desk without releasing his grip on it. 'This is the correct duty statement,' he said.

Stamped in red ink on the top and bottom, in bold capitals, was the word *CONFIDENTIAL*. The text was headed *JOINT*

INTELLIGENCE ORGANISATION. I'd never heard of this branch of government. With all the excitement and anxiety flooding my brain, I had difficulty taking in anything on the paper. I wondered if this was a test of memory under stress, and whether I would pass.

I needn't have feared. That morning's rushed preparation had served me well. I managed to answer his questions and keep my cool.

Despite my interest in the world of spies, stretching back to the geography classroom and my scouting days, I had had no real plan to become an intelligence officer. But now, serendipitously, I was about to be one. For me, the world would become a very different place.

CHAPTER 2

SPY SATELLITES AND YELLOW RAIN

'A man who carries a cat by the tail learns something he can learn in no other way.'

Mark Twain

I was a junior analyst in the Joint Intelligence Organisation's Defence Science and Technical Intelligence directorate, but I had little idea what that meant.

The JIO was Australia's primary assessment body for keeping the government informed of overseas developments of security interest, I soon learned. It also provided strategic intelligence to the various branches of Defence, both military and civilian.

As expected, there was some training on what intelligence involved and how to be an analyst, but mostly the learning was on the job. Robert Mathams – who we always referred to as Mr Mathams in his presence out of respect but as Bob among ourselves – took me under his wing and assigned me the task of monitoring the strategic nuclear competition between the United States and the Soviet Union. This was a relatively new field for Australian intelligence, with a lot of political interest attached, because Australia was involved in the Cold War indirectly, through the joint US–Australian facilities at Pine Gap, Nurrungar and North West Cape.

The work seemed rather strange to me. I could understand gathering intelligence on the Soviet Union, but I was also building files on our close ally, the United States. However, I relished the technical details of the missiles, such as range and accuracy. I played with blast calculators to estimate what nuclear warheads could destroy given distance, height of burst and target hardness.

I struggled with the politics of the Cold War, particularly when it came to the convoluted negotiations on limiting nuclear weapons. Nothing was quite as it seemed. Although both sides said they wanted to restrict and even reduce their nuclear arsenals, their actions seemed in contrast. I expected misleading statements from Leonid Brezhnev, the general secretary of the Communist Party, but not from Richard Nixon, the president of the nation I'd so enjoyed visiting.

There was one proposed treaty, the Strategic Arms Limitation Treaty, between the United States and the Soviet Union that I could never quite get my head around, but it was my duty to monitor and report on it. It was designed to enshrine the concept of mutually assured destruction: if either the United States or the Soviet Union started a nuclear war, each side would be allowed to retain enough nuclear warheads to retaliate with such force that both would be obliterated in the ensuing conflict. The idea was that this would deter open nuclear warfare. With this treaty in place, we could all sleep better at night. At least the acronym, MAD, seemed appropriate to me.

A few years into the job, Bob Mathams decided that my political horizons needed to be broadened and, without my knowledge, arranged a year's study for me at Harvard, in Boston, Massachusetts. I was honoured by his faith in me and more than a little tempted by a chance to live in the United States for a while, but after thinking it over I decided that the politics of the Cold War were not for me. Much to his annoyance, I declined the offer. Another officer was sent instead. Given the circumstances, I felt it only appropriate that I move on, and requested a transfer to the nuclear section, headed by Harry Turner.

This world in some ways was even stranger. Harry – I came to call him by his first name – was a unique individual. He seemed less interested in the work, which was to monitor worldwide nuclear weapons proliferation, than in the investigation of paranormal events and UFOs. Mathams was not thrilled with this, but turned a bit of a blind eye, probably because he thought it a lost cause.

Shortly after I joined, Harry dropped by my office for a chat. We got to talking about how, in the late 1950s and early 1960s, he had attended the British nuclear tests in the desert near Maralinga. He offered hair-raising accounts of things that went wrong. I noticed that Harry was bald, which added an air of veracity to his tales. Then he asked me a question I didn't expect: 'Have you ever had an out-of-body experience?' He explained that on several occasions he had lain on his bed and experienced the sensation of part of himself detaching and floating upwards to look down upon the rest.

I began to wonder if Harry had gotten too close to the tests. I had to confess that this particular sensation was not one I was familiar with.

My answer obviously did not faze him, because he asked me to accompany him to examine the crop circles and scorch marks rumoured to exist in a paddock near Canberra. He was excited by the thought that it could mark a UFO landing.

After a lot of driving around, we could not find the site – nor any visitors from outer space. I doubted that the job description Mathams had so resolutely pulled from my grasp at the interview included this as a key duty.

After a few weeks in his section hunting aliens, Harry asked what I would like to do within his team. Since I had previously been working on US–Soviet strategic treaties, I suggested that perhaps I could work on proliferation treaties.

Harry's nuclear section comprised five experienced scientists and engineers who had been recruited from the United Kingdom because of their knowledge of the nuclear industry. I quickly learned a lot from these men. They had determined between them which areas were of concern and what senior management and other customers might like to know. A couple of these experts specialised in China, while others looked at nuclear-equipped countries of interest to Australia, such as South Africa, India and Pakistan, as well as Indonesia, because it was a close neighbour.

No one in the directorate was looking at the Middle East, so I decided this would become my niche. Although I could not possibly have known it at the time, this decision was to have profound consequences for my future career.

There were no computers then, and our raw intelligence arrived daily, in vast bundles of paper. We would plough through, looking for anything that might be relevant to our territories of interest. When in the depths of a document, I could only wish for a mysterious individual with one pink shoelace, ready to give us the coordinates of every secret nuclear missile base.

Our interactions with other sections, such as the missile researchers, was an important part of our work. This is when we exchanged information on what we had found, or were looking for, and asked if anyone could help. Much of this occurred at our morning and afternoon breaks, when our tea lady, Mrs Page, would wheel in her trolley. We would all stand around sipping our beverages in the vestibule outside our vault, chatting about the latest nuclear developments in India or a recent Chinese missile launch. Mrs Page would often join in the conversation. It was a strange work environment.

Every so often I took trips to the nuclear research establishment at Lucas Heights, south of Sydney. The plant was involved in all aspects of the nuclear fuel cycle, from enrichment of uranium to waste disposal, and it was transformative to visit with my British colleagues and hear their penetrating questions. It's one thing to read about uranium enrichment, quite another to see it in practice. Kilometres of pipework connected the centrifuges, showing the extent of engineering that went into such a plant and the challenges that any nuclear proliferator would face.

I also trained at the then super-secret establishment run by the Australian Secret Intelligence Service (ASIS) on Swan Island, near Queenscliff, Victoria. This was 'spy school'. A small group of us from various Canberra agencies went to the island in Port Phillip Bay for a course on the 'tradecraft' taught to our overseas spies. Much of what we were shown is now outdated, such as secret writing, miniature cameras, and how to forge documents and recognise others' forgeries. It was the stuff of James Bond movies and, to me, absolutely fascinating. One room was set up as a lounge. Microphones and surveillance cameras had been hidden throughout, and we were challenged to find them. We were also briefed on recruiting and running agents, dead-letter drops and various surveillance techniques. Firearms were off the menu: no ASIS officer had a licence to kill.

But I learnt the most when there was an overseas incident that required an assessment by our nuclear team.

In 1979, in an episode that became known as the '22 September event', an ageing American Vela spy satellite detected a double flash of light, each flash separated by milliseconds, in the ocean just south of South Africa. This was characteristic of an atmospheric nuclear explosion. Who could be responsible? And why detonate a large nuclear bomb in the middle of the ocean?

The prime suspect was South Africa. We had been following its nuclear ambitions for some time, and we assessed that it could have enriched enough uranium through a unique process, developed in-country, for at least one bomb. Could this have been a test conducted on a barge off the coast in an effort to avoid detection?

Another candidate was Israel, perhaps testing one of its weapons with the help of South Africa.

We couldn't rule out the possibility that it might all be nothing. The satellite was old, and the flash could be a glitch, perhaps a glint of sun. But it seemed unlikely.

We obtained the print-out from the satellite's computer, but the data was not definitive. More information had to be collected.

I became interested in this event even though it was outside my self-appointed remit of the Middle East. I talked it over with the analyst who specialised in this area, and we decided that if it was an atmospheric test, perhaps someone saw it. After all, it was not far from a busy shipping lane around the Cape. We searched the records and discovered a lone Australian yachtsman whose course had taken him close to the area at about the time of the 'test'. We made enquiries, but he saw nothing exceptional.

If it was an atmospheric test, there would be some nuclear fallout, and McDonald Island, part of the Australian Antarctic Territory, would be in the direct path. Through the Royal Australian Navy, we requested some environmental samples. A few weeks later, I went out to the naval base on the edge of Canberra, HMAS Harman, to collect penguin eggs and moss, still covered with Antarctic ice.

Our colleagues at Lucas Heights examined the samples for traces of the isotopes that might be expected from a nuclear explosion. They found none.

In the face of this evidence, we had to conclude that there had probably not been a nuclear test, although in the intelligence world one can never be absolutely certain. We reported that the double flash recorded by the ageing satellite was most likely a glitch, or perhaps a rare recording of 'super lightning' – most lightning occurs close to the ground, but very occasionally the right sort of clouds form to allow cloud-to-cloud lightning at 15 kilometres or more above the ground. It was possible that the satellite had spotted this.

The event was never solved definitively and is still controversial today. We now know that if there was a nuclear explosion, South Africa was not responsible, as its nuclear weapons program has since been declared and the country was not then in a position to test such a weapon in the South Atlantic. If it was Israel, the logistics of such a test without South Africa's involvement would have been a nightmare. But the possibility of another rogue player is not completely off the table.

For some time, there was not a great deal of government interest in the Middle East: it was too far from our shores. Things changed in September 1980, when Iraqi troops crossed the Iranian border, starting what was to become a debilitating eight-year war. This sparked some federal government interest because of the potential to affect oil supplies and pricing. If timing and relevance were the keys to good intelligence, I could see no better opportunity to write a major report on Iraq's nuclear program. Iraq had ratified the international Treaty on the Non-Proliferation of Nuclear Weapons, and its nuclear research facilities were under safeguard inspection by the International Atomic Energy Agency. But there were certain aspects of its nuclear activities that raised concern, and the scale of its research projects seemed unusually large. Was Iraq obeying the rules? If not, could it soon have nuclear weapons?

It took me some months to collect all the relevant information, so my masterpiece of analysis was not issued until late in May 1981. But on 8 June, about a week after my report was circulated in government circles, news broke that Israel had bombed Iraq's major research facility at Al Tuwaitha, just south of Baghdad. It was an exceptionally clever raid, with Israel's Mirage aircraft flying undetected much of the way while Iraq's attention was focused in the opposite direction, on the threat from Iran. Most of Iraq's key facilities that could have contributed to a nuclear weapons program were destroyed and, along with them, the conclusions in my freshly minted report.

JIO management decided that rather than withdraw my report, we would issue a short addendum summarising the raid and promising a new assessment after the dust had settled. It was a lesson for me on how quickly international situations can change.

I was by now becoming an expert on Middle East nuclear weapons developments, but at the same time I was distracted by a trickle of reports of what were said to be chemical or possibly biological warfare attacks in Laos. At that time, the JIO lacked an analyst with knowledge of chemical or biological warfare, and with my background in biochemistry and microbiology, this seemed a natural fit for me, even though my job was in the nuclear weapons section. Harry, preoccupied with the latest UFO sighting reported by airforce intelligence, seemed unconcerned if I shifted my focus.

The trickle of reports in mid-1981 soon turned into a flood. Australian political interest ramped up when the CIA put out their own assessment, warning that the Soviet Union was supplying chemicals to the Vietnamese for use against rebel groups not just in Laos but also in Cambodia.

The problem for me as an analyst was the confusing array of reports coming in from refugees and resistance fighters. There seemed to be a common theme: a plane would fly over and a rocket would be fired, dispersing a yellow powder that would drift down like rain. After the attack – sometimes immediately, but often days or even weeks later – people would fall ill, with vomiting and diarrhoea the main symptoms. But the reports varied wildly otherwise, and there was very little consistency in the stories.

I needed more information. The obvious course was to collect samples of the chemical and the remains of the munitions that fired it. I also wanted to interview some of the alleged victims directly – much of what we had so far was indirect reporting from aid agencies or journalists. Since Laos and Cambodia were warzones, it would be difficult for me to enter. I tasked my colleagues in ASIS, which collects intelligence overseas, to find someone who could bring back specimens, and at the same time I arranged a trip to Thailand so that I could interview refugees from Laos. This was to be the first of several trips where, with the help of the Australian defence attaché based in Bangkok, I followed the Mekong River, which borders Laos, until it ran into Cambodia, visiting refugee camps along the way and interviewing alleged victims.

By this time, the Americans had obtained their own samples of the yellow powder, and analysis showed that some contained mycotoxins, toxic substances produced by certain species of fungi. I needed to learn more about what the Americans had actually found. What else was in the samples? What was the concentration of toxin? Where had the samples been collected, and what symptoms did they cause? I also had questions about the CIA reports: some things just did not add up. For example, the mycotoxins identified would have caused blindness if even only traces had entered the victims' eyes, but not a single case of blindness had been reported. Yet when questioned through our liaison officer in Washington, the Americans were curiously reticent. Perhaps this was because the United States had recently publicly accused the Soviets of being involved in chemical warfare in Indochina, so the CIA was now being ultra-cautious in what they said.

A high-level delegation was needed to advance the investigation. Bob Mathams had retired, so the new branch head, Dr Maurice Barton, and I, together with a senior Defence Materials Research Laboratories scientist, Dr Hugh Crone, headed to Washington. Our strange task was to investigate the CIA – our key ally's foreign intelligence service – on their findings. By now the issue of Yellow Rain, as it had become known, had been elevated to prime ministerial level, with the US ambassador approaching Malcolm Fraser to request Australia's backing in condemning the Soviets. So our little trio was told not to express our views to the Americans, just collect the sought-after information. At all costs, we were not to utter any reservations about the CIA report, even though we all had serious doubts about its conclusions. So heavily was this drummed into us that when we checked into our Washington hotel, we told the receptionist that we had a 'booking' rather than a 'reservation'. She looked bemused as we chuckled to ourselves at our in-joke.

Our US investigations were more fruitful than we could have imagined. From various sources we found that the level of toxins in the US samples was tiny, not enough to cause harm to humans. Furthermore, only a handful of the samples actually contained any toxin. Even more startling was that most of the material in the samples was pollen! How did this connect to chemical warfare?

Professor Matthew Meselson at Harvard provided an answer. Through private investigation he had discovered what all beekeepers know well: bees often defecate in swarms, and their faeces falls to the ground in sticky droplets like rain. Since a food source for bees is pollen, their droppings are yellow. What the CIA had actually collected was dried bee poo, some of which had become mouldy, perhaps during transit, and so was contaminated with tiny amounts of toxin.

By now ASIS had collected our own yellow powder, and these samples were sent for examination at the Defence Materials Research Laboratories in Melbourne. Sure enough, ours too were bee poo. With the help of Defence scientists, I soon became familiar with its biology, chemistry and morphology. Under a microscope, pollen grains were easily identifiable, although after passing through the digestive tract of a bee, only the outer casings remained. I was now an expert in bee poo: possibly the weirdest qualification I obtained in my career as an intelligence officer.

My investigation at an end, it was time to inform the government of the findings. A colleague from the newly formed Office of National Assessments had recently taken a close interest in the strange case, and together we wrote a comprehensive assessment. We concluded that there had been no chemical warfare in Indochina. The CIA had gotten it dead wrong, probably because it had been influenced by political statements on the issue, made prematurely by the US secretary of state, Alexander Haig (and then his successor, George Shultz), and even the president, Ronald Reagan. In our view, many of the 'chemical victims' had become ill not due to Yellow Rain but to diseases such as dysentery. Others had propagated the story to gain preferential treatment from US officials in the refugee camps. And the samples of the 'chemical agent' were nothing more than bee poo.

Needless to say, the United States was not pleased with our assessment. Almost immediately after receiving a copy of our report, the senior CIA officer in charge of the US investigation wrote a letter to the director of JIO, Garry Marshall, in an attempt to counter our conclusions and perhaps to persuade the Australian government that we had it wrong.

In rather a strange argument, the CIA investigator stated that while specifics of the US research could be challenged, it had to be looked at in its totality. He used the analogy of a mosaic, where tiles are put together to form a picture. I thought this an odd choice. In the intelligence world, assessment is often likened to constructing a jigsaw where some, or even most, of the pieces are missing. The skill of the analyst is to assess what the incomplete picture may look like. Any picture can be made with mosaic tiles, and it seemed to me this was exactly what the CIA had done to support their accusations against the Soviets.

But of greater interest to me was the personal invective. The letter singled me out, as I was the chief investigator on the Australian side, and questioned my objectivity and integrity, concluding that I was 'perverse and mischievous', in an attempt to discredit our findings. The letter would have been career-ending for me if Garry Marshall had taken it seriously; instead, he dismissed it as a last, desperate attempt to change our minds. I was relieved by this, but also perturbed that he didn't think it necessary to attach a counter to the letter before filing it away. I therefore remain labelled in the archives, forever more, as 'perverse and mischievous', without challenge.

The United States did not give up quite so easily. The US ambassador called on Malcolm Fraser in an attempt to persuade him to reject our assessment. To his credit, Fraser was not swayed, telling the ambassador that he trusted his analysts. He did, however, assure the Americans that the Australian government would keep its views to itself to avoid a public stoush.

My Office of National Assessments colleague and I celebrated the end of this long episode with a quiet drink in private. After a glass or two of good red, he joked, 'You know, Rod, all of this was just a plot by the "cagey bees". The KGB was just trying to distract the Americans from more important matters.'

The pun amused me, but also made me ponder the two years of my life spent deep in the poo. Oddly, even to this day, the official US position on the so-called Yellow Rain has not changed. But I have been contacted over the years by several CIA officials who only after retirement felt free to speak their minds, at least to me. They acknowledged that the CIA case had been nonsense. At the time, they said, they had been intimidated by the system from speaking out. The CIA is not an organisation to be easily crossed.

By now, I had truly cut my teeth in the intelligence world. I even promoted myself: I wrote a job description for the head of a new section on chemical and biological warfare, had it approved by Garry Marshall and briefed a fellow officer on what to ask me in the interview. Strange times in a strange occupation.

CHAPTER 3

THE ART OF BIOLOGICAL ANNIHILATION

'Facts do not cease to exist because they are ignored.'

Aldous Huxley

I had much to learn in my new role of monitoring developments in chemical and biological warfare. There was no school for this, and what few books existed tended to be too general and insufficiently technical. The Defence Materials Research Laboratories concentrated on defensive measures against the use of chemical and biological weapons – for example, the development of respirators or means of decontamination. The scientists there were very knowledgeable on the science of these warfare agents, and I visited often, gradually learning the art of poison gas and biological annihilation.

I became aware that the CSIRO was building the Australian National Animal Health Laboratories. The laboratories were designed to handle harmful animal diseases, including those that could pose a danger to humans, such as anthrax. Although this state-of-the-art facility was designed for a peaceful purpose, it occurred to me that any country trying to disguise a biological warfare program may have something similar. I decided to pay a visit to look at the layout and pipework.

This was an ideal time to visit, since the facility was almost complete but not yet operational, so there was no restriction on where I could go. It stretched across five levels, with the middle level housing the laboratories, the upper two purifying exhaust air and the lower two decontaminating liquid waste. I was particularly interested in its external appearance, since in satellite imagery this is all an analyst might see of a similar foreign facility that may be housing something more sinister.

I also wanted to see the production equipment that could be used to make biological agents such as anthrax. I arranged a visit to the Commonwealth Serum Laboratories near Melbourne. CSL did not make biological weapons, of course, but they did produce vaccines in small fermenters, and something similar would have been quite useful to countries with a more evil intent. But this also demonstrated the intelligence analyst's dilemma: how to distinguish between a fermenter that has been imported to make vaccines to save people's lives and one that has been imported to make anthrax to kill people.

As I was learning the tradecraft of a chemical and biological warfare expert, a situation emerged in Iraq. The disastrous war Iraq had started with Iran in 1980 had become bogged in a type of trench warfare not dissimilar to that seen in World War I. It had become a war of attrition, in which the mathematics were stacked against Iraq, because of its smaller population. In 1983, my attention was drawn to a large, clearly secure facility being built in the middle of the desert, 100 kilometres northwest of Baghdad. This was no animal health laboratory, but a chemical plant. Yet was it a chemical weapons facility or a soap factory?

Intelligence began to roll in that Iraq was ordering large quantities of particular chemicals. I realised, based on what I had recently learnt about chemical weapons, that these were the raw ingredients for the production of mustard gas. The clincher on what the factory in the desert was for came when, through other intelligence, I was able to link the imports directly to that facility. There was now no doubt in my mind that it was a chemical weapons plant.

This disturbing finding was a significant development amid an already devastating war. A special briefing for senior military and Defence policy officers was set up in the Joint Intelligence Organisation's theatre. A written version was circulated to other government officers, such as those in foreign affairs.

I had prepared well for the briefing, and went through my investigations step-by-step, explaining the science of mustard gas production in terms my audience would understand. My conclusions were that Iraq had made mustard gas and that we could expect they would soon deploy it in the war with Iran.

But when I finished my presentation, I was met with silence. The air of disbelief weighed heavily. Finally, a major general in the front row shifted in his seat and, struggling to find the right phrasing so as not to offend me, said, 'Mustard gas was a World War I weapon and has not been used since. Why would Iraq bother with an obsolete weapon?'

He was right, of course – mustard gas had not been used in more than seventy years. But in World War I it had proven very effective in trench warfare, flushing out soldiers, and that was the type of war Iraq was now fighting. I felt that the evidence for my conclusions was overwhelming. The science and the intelligence don't lie, I told the general.

Only a couple of months later, any doubts my audience may have had were dispelled. The first reports of chemical attacks drifted in, much as I had predicted. These were substantiated by the Iranian government's release of horrific photographs of victims with yellowish, fluid-filled blisters on their bodies. The injuries were characteristic of mustard gas burns.

The question now for Australia, and the international community, was what to do about these chemical warfare attacks. But while all this was being debated in the United Nations, the frequency of the mustard gas attacks increased. Perhaps even more disturbingly, it appeared from pictures Tehran released that an even deadlier gas, the nerve agent sarin, was now also being used. This too I had predicted. Intelligence reports had indicated that Iraq had begun to import the precursor chemicals to make sarin and some other types of nerve agents from Europe. By early 1985 Iraq had started to kill hundreds, and later it would be thousands, of Iranian soldiers with its use of sarin.

As expected, the United Nations condemned Iraq for its use of chemical warfare, but that made little difference to a country in a desperate battle against an enemy the Iraqi leaders considered barely human. Something more substantial than Security Council condemnation was needed to stop Iraq.

A key purpose of foreign intelligence is to enable politicians to influence geopolitical events to produce a more favourable outcome for a nation and its allies. Australia could have done nothing and simply left it to others, but advisers in the Department of Foreign Affairs, acting on our assessments, put it to the foreign minister, Bill Hayden, that Australia should organise a meeting of countries supplying Iraq to restrict the sale of chemicals. He agreed. Thus in 1985 Australia hosted the first meeting of fifteen countries, held in Belgium, followed by meetings in Australia's more spacious Paris embassy. In recognition of Australia's initiative, it became known as the Australia Group.

For the first time, I could see that intelligence could influence policy in a positive way. Through the Australia Group, the world became safer. Unlike the pyrrhic victory over the CIA, which merely made me feel good in uncovering a truth, the intelligence on Iraq's acquisition of chemical weapons delivered tangible results. Although none of us could have foreseen it, this multilateral group went on to expand and strengthen, and today is one of the main mechanisms to control dual-use materials and equipment that could contribute to chemical and biological weapon programs.

An intelligence exchange was also held in conjunction with each Australia Group policy meeting. I became Australia's representative at these. Through an intelligence-sharing arrangement with the United States, the United Kingdom and Canada, I had attended intelligence exchanges in Washington, London and Ottawa, but the Paris meetings were different. The participating countries were not all natural bedfellows, and at the inaugural exchange in 1985 there was a certain awkwardness as we sat around a long table in a secure room in the centre of the Australian embassy. Participants from Italy, France, Japan, Germany, Australia, the United Kingdom and others eyed one another, feeling exposed as we revealed ourselves as intelligence officers for nations once rivals, but at the same time curious about what scraps of information we might collect. There was a lot of note-scribbling that day.

Through the Australia Group I gained further insights into the world of chemical and biological weapons proliferation. I developed an understanding of the devious means by which some countries purchased and imported chemicals and equipment: I learnt about front countries, middlemen, false end-user certificates and other tricks to circumvent controls on exports of technology. This education was particularly valuable in knowing what to look for in incoming intelligence reports.

It soon became clear to me that monitoring worldwide chemical and biological warfare developments was a job for more than one person, particularly with my Australia Group obligations. I went to Maurice Barton, the branch head, and suggested that a section be created to do just this. He agreed. Proliferation studies, PS, was formed, incorporating the former nuclear section and an expanded focus on chemical and biological warfare. I was to head it.

I was gradually climbing the intelligence ladder.

* * *

Shortly after becoming the head of proliferation studies, I received a visit from an ASIS colleague. A Russian scientist attending a conference in Sydney had jumped ship and was seeking asylum. According to ASIS, he was no ordinary scientist, but had been working on a secret biological warfare program for the Soviet regime. Could I interview him to determine if he was telling the truth?

Under the Five Eyes alliance – an intelligence-sharing agreement between the United States, the United Kingdom, Canada, New Zealand and Australia – monitoring Russian activities was usually the province of the United States and the United Kingdom, and well over half their intelligence resources were devoted to this task; Australia's direct interest was minor. But since we exchanged intelligence with our Five Eyes partners, here was a chance, perhaps, to contribute something original.

The next day, I was in Sydney in a hotel room with an intelligence officer from ASIS and another from ASIO. We introduced ourselves and discussed a plan of attack. The ASIS officer told us that the Russian scientist, 'Dimitri', was being held in a safe house in the Western suburbs, and the ASIS officer would lead us there via a circuitous route to ensure we were not being followed. I was to ask Dimitri the questions, and the other two would say they were my friends. This ruse seemed a little bizarre to me – after all, why would I bring friends along? – but I went along with it. The ASIS officer also insisted we should adopt pseudonyms. I became Dave, while my 'friends' were Jason and Mike.

I half-expected an Aston Martin in the hotel carpark, so James Bond–like all this was, but there was just a rented Toyota. We set off down side streets, and a few times stopped abruptly, reversed and set off in another direction. I wasn't sure if our ASIS friend was lost or just acting like 007; either way, it would have confused anyone trying to follow us.

Eventually we arrived at the safe house, and after a few minutes of scanning the street, we determined that we hadn't been followed by the KGB. We left the car to enter a run-down townhouse.

Inside, Dimitri and his ASIS minder were sitting at a dilapidated table in the kitchen. Dimitri stood up and I shook his hand. 'Greetings, Dimitri,' I said. 'I am looking forward to our chat. I'm Dave.' Waving my hand towards one of my companions, I added, 'This is a friend of mine, Jason.' Almost immediately I remembered his pseudonym was Mike, but now I had to continue with my faux pas. I gestured to my other colleague and said, 'And this is another friend, Mike.' My 'friends' winced slightly but had no choice but to go along with it.

Dimitri was in his early thirties, spoke good English and seemed very self-composed. After some small talk, I got around to asking him about himself. He had studied genetics and biochemistry at Moscow State University, where he had met his wife, a librarian. Dimitri obtained a government research position and was transferred to an institute in Koltsovo, Siberia. He and his wife lived in the nearby city of Novosibirsk, where their child was born.

I had never heard of Koltsovo. I discovered later that it was a small 'closed' location – a place where no outsiders were permitted unless on official duties. It was one of many such sites during the Soviet era.

I spoke with Dimitri for a couple of hours, over coffee served by Jason – or was it Mike? Mike also got our pseudonyms confused, and at one stage even called me Rod. We were beginning to look less like smooth MI6 operators and more like characters from *Get Smart*. Dimitri did not seem to notice or, if he did, he played it cool: he was either a very good double agent or he was who he said he was – a scared junior scientist who had defected.

I knew I needed to interview Dimitri again, after I had researched the institute he said he worked for. I arranged a follow-up through ASIS; this time, the interview would be in Canberra.

A few weeks later, we met again at a safe house in an inner Canberra suburb. As before, the agents and I went through dramatic route changes to get there. We used the same revised pseudonyms: Mike was Jason and Jason was Mike. I now knew, through liaising with the CIA, that the *naukograd* (science town) of Koltsovo was potentially involved in the Soviet biological warfare program. The institute Dimitri worked for was suspected of developing genetically engineered pathological biological weapons agents – for example, a new strain of anthrax could be engineered to be resistant to antibiotics except for one the Soviets had made in secret.

My objective was to determine exactly what building in Koltsovo Dimitri worked in. I had drawn a map of the town using top-secret satellite imagery. Russia had forbidden private citizens from having maps of that area, and this was the first time Dimitri had seen one. He was fascinated. He pored over the map for a few minutes, and then, with a confused look, said, 'I am not sure.'

'That's okay,' I replied, 'but let's go through this step-by-step. You caught the train from Novosibirsk every day, right?'

He nodded.

I pointed to the railway line I had drawn on my sketch and said, 'Here is the Koltsovo railway station. When you arrived here, which way did you turn?'

Painstakingly, we worked out his route through the streets together. Eventually he pointed to a building and, looking me dead in the eye, said confidently, 'I am sure it is this one.'

As a junior scientist, Dimitri did not have a great deal to contribute to our understanding of the Soviet biological weapons program. But the identification of one building was a very small piece in a much larger jigsaw.

A short while later, I was in Washington on JIO business. Although I had no plans to visit the CIA, they were apparently keen to see me, and a request came through that I should drop by – a bit of an about-face from my Yellow Rain days. At CIA headquarters, Langley, I sat round a table with three biological warfare analysts. The leader of the group, whom we'll call Sara, said, 'We have seen a summary of your report on Dimitri. For about a year now we have had our own intel reports about genetic engineering at Koltsovo, but nothing definite. We don't even know what building might be a candidate for the work.' I could see them all looking at me with eager faces as Sara continued, 'What more can you tell us?'

We discussed the subject for the next half-hour, and then Sara slipped from her folder some very high-quality satellite photos of Koltsovo. It took me a few moments to orient myself. Then I stabbed the picture with my finger. 'That's it, there!' I said, recalling the convoluted path I had traced with Dimitri.

I heard one of the analysts mutter under her breath, 'I knew it.'

Sara simply said, 'Thank you. Thank you, Rod.'

This tiny scrap of intelligence stood me in good stead with the CIA. They now had an answer on something they had been puzzling over for some time. Perhaps I had redeemed myself just a little in their eyes.

CHAPTER 4

LONDON CALLING

'As a general rule, the most successful man in life is the man who has the best information.'

Benjamin Disraeli

'Well, Mr Barton, tell us what you consider to be the most important attributes of an overseas intelligence liaison officer.'

This wasn't a question I was expecting, and in my confusion I stumbled over a reply. 'Honesty and hard-working. And, oh, er, obviously an understanding of how allied agencies are organised and operate.'

I was already berating myself as the words spilled out to the job selection panel that included the director of JIO, Garry Marshall, and his deputy, David Mannett. Why did I say 'honesty'? I could see David grimace at its mention. Although the panel might not acknowledge it, subterfuge and cunning were more important attributes.

JIO had an intelligence liaison officer stationed in London and one in Washington. Their job was to keep in close contact with intelligence agencies and channel information back to headquarters in Canberra. Often they gathered information in response to specific requests from Canberra, but there was nothing to stop a liaison officer from just trawling for items that might interest analysts back home. More mundane duties included arranging visits from analysts or other officials. Both positions were highly coveted, so when the positions became due for renewal towards the end of 1986, there was a rush of applicants.

I too decided to apply, but only for the London job, largely because London is an excellent jumping-off point to see the places in Europe I hadn't managed to visit on my previous stay. And after my run-in with the CIA over Yellow Rain, I still might not be entirely welcome in all Washington quarters. After all, would the Americans want to spill secrets to someone they had described as 'perverse and mischievous'?

A few weeks after my shaky interview, I was invited into Garry Marshall's office and told the good news that I was the best person for the Washington job. Marshall explained it was the more important of the two liaison positions, and the organisation wanted someone with my knowledge and depth of experience (by that, I assumed he did not just mean in bee poo).

I was flattered, but also slightly deflated: I hadn't even applied for Washington. I steeled myself for a difficult conversation.

But Marshall continued: on reflection, the selection panel thought that if I was posted to Washington, 'this might send the wrong message to the CIA'. So I would be appointed as the liaison officer to the UK Defence Intelligence Staff in London instead. My new role as the Australian Defence Intelligence Liaison Officer – with the fancy acronym of ADILO – would begin in just over a month's time, in November 1986.

Marshall showed me a letter he had received from the incumbent, whom we'll call Luke Cavendish. The letter surveyed his almost three years in London and lamented that there had not been enough work to keep him occupied; the number of requests from JIO analysts seeking information from the Defence Intelligence Staff were few. What rankled the director was Cavendish's recommendation that the position be downgraded and used as a training role.

There was an element of truth in the observations: the London job was certainly less busy than the Washington job. However, as Marshall pointed out, it was still vital we were represented there at an appropriate level, as the United Kingdom was an important ally and often had sources and material of great interest to us. His concern was that if the policymakers in Defence saw Cavendish's recommendation, the bean counters elsewhere in the department might use this as a reason to cut the position altogether.

So he gave me a stern warning: if I did not make the job work, I might be the last ADILO in London.

I received very little training for or direction about the job; it was assumed that I would work out what was required once there. Yet there was a general course run by the Department of Foreign Affairs that all appointees to Defence positions overseas were required to attend. It related to protocol, diplomacy and etiquette. For example, if invited to a dinner party at 7.00 pm, at what time would it be appropriate to arrive? Being a punctual person, I would of course arrive at 7.00. But the answer is not so simple, we learnt; for instance, in some South American countries, turning up a couple of hours late might be quite acceptable. In London, ten minutes late is the accepted protocol, as it gives the host and hostess that little bit of extra time to double-check that all the cutlery on the table is in the correct order. After all, no one wants to see a melon fork out of place.

This instruction in manners was balanced against weightier matters. One thing I had not given a moment's thought to was that, as an intelligence officer in a foreign country, I needed to be exceptionally careful. In this role, being arrested in some countries might mean I would be shot as a spy. I was assured that I would be issued with a diplomatic passport, which would help to get me out of any jams that should arise when I travelled outside the United Kingdom.

I arrived in London on a misty morning in late November 1986. I was soon to become the conduit for intelligence flowing back to Canberra, but I still lacked a clear idea of how I was to operate on a day-to-day basis. As helpful as it was to know what time to turn up to a dinner party, it had not quite prepared me for the job.

My office wasn't located in Australia House, with the other diplomatic staff, but in the midst of the Defence Intelligence Staff, near the heart of the British government. I realised this would be very convenient, not only because I wouldn't have to traipse back and forth, but because it would be easier to develop a rapport with the British analysts.

The day after my long flight, I made my way to a classic Victorian building, the Metropole on Northumberland Avenue, where my office was located on the third floor. Most of the Defence Intelligence Staff were housed in this building, and the rest, including the Chief of Defence Intelligence, were in the main Defence complex in Whitehall, just a short walk away. The Metropole Building was once the Metropole Hotel, an upmarket residence by the late nineteenth century. During World War I it had been requisitioned by the British War Office and, in the way of these matters, never returned. It had a lot of history: Winston Churchill had his office here when he was the Minister of Munitions. And the rumour was that my office, including the outer office where my personal assistant worked, had been previously used for liaison of a different kind between Edward VII and one of his mistresses.

Now, however, the building was a creaking mess. Years of neglect had seen this grand place sag to near ruin. Everything needed repair: the plumbing, heating, wiring, staircases. The once-elegant marble entrances had at some stage been painted grey or brown – it was hard to tell which – and the paint was peeling. The chandeliers in the ballroom had been replaced with fluorescent lights, but at least the oak panelling had not been painted over, as it had in much of the rest of the building. I suppose it could be said that the Metropole still had character, of a kind.

The handover with Cavendish was brief. He was packing up to return to Australia in a hurry. On my first morning, we made lightning calls on the heads of about twenty branches, and in the afternoon we dashed over to the main building to meet the chief, his deputies, his assistants and their assistants. Then off to Australia

House, where I was introduced to the Australian high commissioner, his deputy, the head of the Australian Defence Staff, and other senior personnel and their assistants. By the end of the day, I had met more than 100 people. My head was spinning.

'I'll introduce you to the heads of other areas in DIS tomorrow,' Cavendish said.

'How many are there?' I asked, with trepidation.

'Oh, about another forty branches. But you'll have to introduce yourself to the section heads and their staff, and of course to the administrative staff.'

I discovered that in all there would be more than 700 people I needed to know – and as the liaison officer, I would have to learn their names quickly. This was a job about people.

Remembering names wasn't something I was ever very good at. However, at spy school I had learnt about mnemonics, and here it proved useful. Mnemonics is a system of word association, so I might remember a Mr Jones with a clue like 'Indiana', or a Mr Wright as 'not wrong'. With this system, it usually took a few moments for the cogs in my brain to turn to the right setting. I had to be careful not to get the system backwards and call Mr Nelson 'Horatio', for example. But using mnemonics, I was soon able to remember about 500 names, and I just winged the rest.

After the second morning, that was it: I was flying solo. Well, except for my personal assistant, Penny, who could advise me on some of the intricacies of the job and who some of the Brits were when they popped by the office. Unfortunately, Penny had agreed to stay on only for a handover, and within a couple of days she too would be gone. To save money, JIO would not send out another assistant from Australia, but advised me to recruit locally. It was all a major headache. Because of the sensitive material I would be collecting, my assistant had to be an Australian, trustworthy and capable, and needed security clearances to Top Secret level, a procedure that normally took months.

To seek help with recruiting the right assistant, I decided that my first visit would be to my Australian counterpart in ASIO, whom we'll call Mark Hawkins. His job concerned matters that affected Australia's internal security, such as terrorism and counter-espionage, whereas my role in the JIO was to deal with matters external to Australia, but there was often overlap in our duties. Back in Canberra I had often worked with ASIO and knew Mark from those times. Since he had been in London for a couple of years, I thought he might know where to find a reliable personal assistant.

Mark's office in Australia House seemed vaguely familiar. Perhaps this was where I had been briefed sixteen years earlier, when I was a patent examiner embarking on my Russian adventure.

I explained my dilemma.

Mark replied, 'You might be in luck, Rod. Until recently we had a woman working for us here, but she had to return to Australia a couple of months ago, when her husband's posting at the High Commission finished.'

I was wondering how someone in Australia would be of any use to me in London when Mark added, 'Her husband's just been reposted to London. We'd have liked her to come back to work for us, but we've already found a replacement. If you'd like to interview her, I can arrange it. And, by the way, she still has all the necessary clearances. Her name is Jan.'

Mark also said that he might be able to help me with another problem. I wondered what he meant. Did I have other problems?

He showed me half a dozen boxes stacked in the corner of his office. This was booze left over from another ASIO officer who had recently returned to Australia, he explained. 'You can have this at half-price – all duty-free, of course. Just take the cost out of your entertainment allowance. With Christmas coming up, you're going to need it.'

This was a problem I could handle.

I headed back to my office in Whitehall in a chauffeur-driven embassy car with the boot full of booze. Penny was there to greet me, and I warned her to expect a delivery, which was on its way up.

'You'll need this then.' She handed me two keys and pointed me to a double-doored steel cabinet on the wall opposite my desk. I had noticed it earlier and wondered what was inside. Not only were the doors equipped with a substantial lock, but there was also a heavy padlock keeping the contents secure. Perhaps this was where dark secrets were kept. I opened the cabinet in great expectation – only to find half a bottle of cheap red on the otherwise empty shelves. Mark was either prescient or he knew Cavendish too well!

Cavendish had actually warned me to get some Scotch in. After saying farewell, he doubled back to pop his head around the door.

'Sorry, I forgot to warn you about Allan Shore. He'll be down to see you soon. He likes the occasional drink.'

Allan had been the British intelligence liaison officer in Canberra. He was an extrovert, a cross, perhaps, between Rumpole of the Bailey and an old-timey sea captain. In fact, he had once been an officer in the Royal Navy, and maybe this is where he had picked up a formidable drinking habit – nothing about waiting for the sun to pass over the yardarm for him.

I only had a short wait that morning before Allan burst into my office, uttered some expletive, called me an old bastard by way of greeting and sat down looking for his morning fix of whisky. I had just finished stacking my cabinet, so we both enjoyed a little tipple, all in the spirit of good liaison work.

The morning's drink was only the start. Cavendish had mentioned that I was fortunate it was almost Christmas. I'd agreed: 'Ah, a short break before I start the real work.' That was not what he meant. He explained that I would be invited to Christmas parties, which would be ideal for introductions.

I thought some of my training might come in handy – at least I would know when to arrive. But I was puzzled. 'Why would anyone invite me? I've only just landed in the country. No one knows me.'

Cavendish explained patiently, 'They may not know you, but they know who you are.' He added, 'The DIS is cutting down on parties this year, so there'll only be about thirty-five.'

And so, a couple of days after my handover, I started the party circuit. On the first day of the season I attended three parties: a long and boozy lunchtime affair, and two in the evening, all held for the sake of convenience in Whitehall government offices. By the time I got home I was a wreck. I had indigestion from all the vol-au-vents and little unidentified things on sticks. I had also drunk far too much and was queasy. I could hardly remember whom I had met, let alone what they had said. With another thirty-two parties to go, I worried that I might not survive to Christmas. Parties were meant to be fun, but this was a nightmare.

The next morning, I came to the solemn realisation that this was part of the job. I was being paid to party. I needed a more professional approach, and a few rules: do not eat the food, no alcohol, and always carry a pen and notebook. The last was a habit that I adopted for the rest of my working life.

At the next party, as I sipped a gin and tonic minus the gin, I politely declined the little things on sticks, listened carefully to my hosts and casually asked questions about their work. At appropriate intervals, I would go to the men's room, sit in a cubicle and jot down who was who and what I had learned. This would form the basis of my reports to Canberra the next day.

I also hosted my own parties, over the festive season and throughout the year. These were usually held in my office and had an Australian theme, including Vegemite sangers – from which I removed the crusts, in accordance with my protocol training. Jan was vital in coordinating and preparing the invitations, and added a touch of sophistication to these gatherings while at the same time saving money so that every penny of my entertainment allowance was well spent. Any food remaining, I would give to the homeless living under the arches at a tube station near to the Metropole. I wondered what commuters made of it as they scurried past these men and women dining on vol-au-vents.

But the best parties were under the main building of the Ministry of Defence, in a wine cellar that was once part of Henry VIII's palace. The palace had been burnt to the ground by some great fire, and the cellar long forgotten. After World War II, it was discovered during the excavation of the foundations for a new Defence building. It had been beautifully restored, and its vaulted ceilings made it a great function room, albeit buried in the second basement of one of London's most secure buildings. It was here I held wine tastings of some of the best Australian reds. I pondered what Henry would have thought of us in his cellar, drinking wine from a country he had never heard of.

Although officially I was JIO's 'man in London', Canberra sometimes sent me on assignments beyond the capital. Most of these were to attend weapons exhibitions or air shows, such as those at Farnborough or Paris. My task was to collect brochures of new military equipment that might be sold to countries in Australia's sphere of interest and gather information, such as technical specifications and likely production dates, from the sales representatives. If asked, my cover was that I was a representative of the Australian Defence department dealing with equipment acquisition, and to back that up my business card stated that I was a *Counsellor of Defence, Australian High Commission, London.*

One of my trips was to a relatively minor military trade expo in Lisbon in 1987. I was waiting outside my hotel, the Turim, for a taxi to take me to the venue on the outskirts of town when a well-dressed man waddled out of the hotel and stood beside me. Looking at the expo pass on my lanyard, he asked in very good English, with an eastern European inflection, 'Can I give you a lift?' Showing his own pass, he added, 'I too am going to the expo. My limo will arrive soon.'

Frustrated at the lack of cabs, I gratefully accepted. As we settled into the plush back seats of the vehicle, I sized him up. He was portly, and his clothing looked expensively tailored. He wore a profusion of jewellery, with several rings, a thick gold chain bracelet on his right wrist and what looked like a Breitling watch on his left. I could only sum him up as: sleazy.

He volunteered, 'I am Laszlo Vitov. I am a weapons broker.'

'That must be fascinating work,' I replied. 'I work for the Australian government.'

'What do you do?' he asked.

I gave him the usual answer: 'Defence acquisition.'

He boasted, 'Anything you want to buy, I can arrange. I have many contacts in many countries. They sell me helicopters, guns, missiles, anything. Anything, I can get it.'

I felt a little outside my comfort zone with this revelation, so I turned the conversation to small talk. But as we stepped out of the car at the expo, he said, 'Would you like to meet in the Turim's lounge this evening for drinks?'

I was reluctant to be in his company for a protracted stretch.

Yet he seemed like the type who might yield some useful intel, so I graciously agreed.

That evening, I ordered a Portuguese tempranillo while Vitov had a Scotch and soda.

'So, you work in acquisition,' Vitov said. 'Are you also involved in sales?'

'Not really,' I replied. 'Why do you ask?'

'I understand that Australia has Mirage aircraft that are no longer needed. I might have a buyer.'

It was true that the Australian Mirages were soon to be replaced by F/A-18 Hornets, and I had confidential information that Pakistan was interested in the Mirages, but I was not going to reveal that. 'Well, sales are not really my field,' I said carefully, while wondering who he had in mind as the buyer. I added, 'Their sale might be tricky. The Australian government would not want to upset any regional balances.'

Much to my surprise, he replied, 'Pakistan is not the buyer I have in mind.' He could clearly see dollars in any sale he could arrange, and eventually he revealed Yemen as the potential buyer. I was not sure I believed him on this – or, for that matter, on anything. He probably distrusted me, too; such was the business we were in.

Before parting ways, he handed me his business card, which identified him as a 'broker of trade goods', with an office at an address in Belgrade. 'If you need any help on this matter, contact me,' he said.

That was the last I saw of Vitov. But his intelligence proved handy.

By early 1987, I had built up quite a range of contacts in the British intelligence services, and these soon proved valuable.

On 14 May, Colonel Sitiveni Rabuka ousted the Fijian government in a military coup. Australia was concerned, given our close ties with Fiji, and this concern increased a few months later when a shipment of weapons, uniforms and other military items was intercepted in Cairns. The shipment had originated from a Mediterranean port and was labelled as farm machinery; it was intended to be sent onwards to Fiji. It included twenty or thirty AK-47 assault rifles, the weapon of choice for many armies, resistance fighters and terrorists. Canberra asked, could the British help us in determining where had they originated, who they were for and whether more shipments were on the way?

There is a branch of intelligence in which the British excel: the study of markings on munitions. All the guns in the Fiji shipment had serial numbers and other markings, and from these I assumed the Brits could tell me exactly where and when they were made. I dropped in on the branch head, Andrew Watkins, and as a negotiating tactic I decided to tell him about the arms dealer I had met in Lisbon just a few weeks earlier. 'His name is Laszlo Vitov,' I said.

I could see I had Watkins' interest by the way he leaned slightly forward across the desk. I related Vitov's interest in the Mirages and his alleged client, the Yemenis.

Hesitantly, Watkins said, 'Yes … we know of Vitov. He is a petty weapons dealer mainly supplying arms to the Middle East. These deals are usually legal, as he sells to governments.' But then, even more hesitantly, he added in a low tone, 'We think he might also be implicated in the sale of weapons to Hezbollah.'

It sounded to me like Vitov was probably more than 'implicated'. I decided to play the ace up my sleeve. 'I have his business card,' I said, and flashed it. 'Would you like a copy?'

Watkins gratefully accepted, and asked, more as a courtesy than anything else, 'Would you mind if I shared it with our colleagues at MI6?'

I knew that the contact details on the card might be useful to other British intelligence services and, of course, I readily agreed.

In return, Watkins was more than happy to provide me with intelligence on the weapons headed to Fiji. It turned out they had been made three years earlier in a Czechoslovakian factory, under licence from the Soviet Union, and had been sold to the Libyan National Army.

All this Watkins was relaxed in telling me, but he became evasive with my questions about how he thought the weapons had reached Australia. He started to interrogate me on what else I knew of the shipments. British intelligence had little interest in Fiji generally, but in this case, for reasons he was not revealing, Watkins was acutely interested in the small cache of weapons seized in Cairns.

I joked that he would not be invited to my next office party unless he told all. Watkins contemplated whether to say more.

What came next was a fascinating story.

The serial numbers of the AK-47s destined for Fiji overlapped with those they believed had been acquired illegally by a Jordanian arms dealer, he said. This was a small part of a large Libyan order that had never reached that country, perhaps due to bribery or theft.

British intelligence had tracked the weapons through several countries until they had been loaded onto a Greek ship. Most of these weapons had been headed for Northern Ireland, but UK Special Forces had intercepted the shipment before it reached its destination. The fate of the remainder of the weapons had been unknown to them until now. With the discovery in Cairns, most were now accounted for.

In hushed tones, Watkins confided in me, 'Look, I have to be careful what I say here, and please keep this to yourself. We now know who the arms dealer is and we are closing in on him. And by the way, it's not Vitov. But the last thing we want is a bunch of Australians with hobnailed boots trampling over our patch.'

I assured him that we would keep out of his patch even in sneakers. I thanked him for being so candid.

Of course, next I did what any professional intelligence liaison officer would have done. I raced to my office. In my report to Canberra, I advised extreme caution on how the intelligence was to be used; certainly no hobnailed boots.

I was still very mindful of Garry Marshall's warning to 'make the job work', and over time I actively sought out intelligence that would interest Canberra. I spent a lot of mornings knocking on doors, 'casually chatting' with analysts and then scurrying back to my office to write down what I had learnt before I forgot the detail. As a professional, I had to be subtle in all of this, as too much probing would be counterproductive in the long run. Nevertheless, the flow of intelligence back to Australia dramatically improved, and I was loving the job.

At functions hosted by the Brits, or by my American and Canadian counterparts, I polished my tradecraft. Sometimes, especially after a few drinks, someone would drop hints about intelligence they were working on, and I would casually call in on them in the following days to chase up on the lead.

One cocktail party was hosted by the CIA in the US embassy. Senior British intelligence officers from the DIS, MI5 and MI6 were invited and, for good measure, I was too. On entering the room, it was obvious that the CIA liaison officer had a far larger entertainment allowance than me. Waiters, immaculately dressed and carrying cocktails and canapes, twirled through the crowd, who mingled around a decorative pool, complete with elegant aquatic plants, in the centre of the lobby. No Vegemite sangers in sight.

I soon found myself engaged in a conversation about the *Titanic* with the CIA liaison officer and a senior MI6 official. As the MI6 officer explained animatedly how the *Titanic* had sunk, he inadvertently stepped backwards, into the decorative pool, sinking up to his shins. Amazingly, he did not miss a beat. With champagne glass still in hand, he continued his explanation, before casually stepping out as if nothing had happened, tuxedo pants dripping. The sinking of the *Titanic* was a little outdated to report back to Canberra, but I was impressed with his nonchalance. Clearly, British manners were crucial to intelligence in this milieu.

* * *

As an Australian representative, I was invited to DIS intelligence meetings on specific topics. Often, the subject matter was of little interest to Australia – for example, a debt crisis in Peru or the forthcoming Albanian elections. But in early 1988, one topic arose that had great relevance to Australian interests.

In March of that year, Kurdish refugees from northern Iraq reported that chemical weapons had been used against them in the town of Halabja, near the Iranian border. The reports indicated that hundreds, if not thousands, had been killed, many of them women and children. This sparked an investigation by British intelligence: by 1988 it was well documented that Iraq had been using chemical weapons in its war with Iran, but this was the first time that the weapons had been reported in use against a civilian population.

The event was significant enough for the UK chief of defence intelligence to authorise a national assessment report, to be delivered to senior cabinet ministers and the prime minister, Margaret Thatcher. The DIS, in conjunction with Cabinet Assessment Staff (CAS), drafted the report, which would be considered by all the intelligence chiefs at a Joint Intelligence Committee (JIC) meeting. Representatives of 'the Allies' – the United States, Canada and Australia – were also invited.

Attendance at JIC meetings fell to the Australian Office of National Assessments liaison officer. However, when he was absent, which was often, I took his place. I enjoyed attending the meetings largely because I was fascinated by their formality and ritual, which seemed to me a throwback to the days of the British Empire.

The meetings were held in offices adjacent to the chambers of the Privy Council in Whitehall. The oak-panelled room had subdued lighting and plush carpets. Sombre portraits of long-forgotten dignitaries stared down. The seating order was precise, with the chairman, Sir Percy Craddock, seated at the head of the very long table. The room had only one window, and Sir Percy was sat prudently with his back to it: this window overlooked 10 Downing Street, and the joke was that occasionally Mrs Thatcher could be seen hanging out the washing on the line. At the far end to Sir Percy were 'the Allies', with representatives from – from right to left as seen by Sir Percy – the CIA, the DIA, Canada and Australia. Perhaps the order indicated our relative importance, or our political persuasion. The heads of the British intelligence agencies, among them MI5, MI6 and GCHQ (the Government Communications Headquarters, responsible for electronic signal intercepts), sat in their designated positions around the table, with the chief of defence intelligence, as deputy chair, next to Sir Percy. Members of the CAS were seated along the sides of the room, ready to take notes and provide papers as required.

The assessment was introduced by the head of the CAS, who briefly outlined recent events and the reason for the paper. Sir Percy made some preliminary comments expressing the seriousness of the developments and the interest Prime Minister Thatcher had shown in the subject. Next, he elicited comment from those sitting around the table, keeping to a strict protocol of speaking order. On reaching the head of MI5, he looked over his glasses and, in his plummy accent, asked, 'Perhaps C may be able to enlighten us?'

It puzzled me that he always referred to him as C when everyone around the table knew him well: he was Sir Antony Duff. Much later, I learnt that this was a tradition, and that 'C' stood for chief, as in the chief of MI5. The chief of MI6, however, was referred to by his actual name, Sir Christopher Curwen – so apparently no tradition there.

This was not the first time the JIC had deliberated on Iraq and its weapons of mass destruction; nor would it be the last. I was impressed by the quality of the discussion. The emphasis was on whether the findings were backed by enough evidence. Rarely in the intelligence world does one gain absolute proof; in any assessment, the considerations relate to the reliability of sources, the consistency between various types of sources, and the existence, or otherwise, of contradictory evidence. The JIC debated these aspects. The interpretation of all the evidence was then picked apart. Finally, Sir Percy suggested some changes to phrasing – nuances to more accurately reflect the nature of the evidence and to show the level of confidence the committee had in its conclusions. The central conclusion was that the evidence pointed overwhelmingly to Iraq having used a chemical weapon, probably nerve gas, against the Kurds in the north of the country, in what seemed part of a larger campaign against this ethnic minority.

Little did I think this subject would come to affect my life significantly. I would spend many years caught up with it. But when it came to my turn to speak at that meeting, having had no instructions from Canberra, all I could say was, 'Australia has nothing to add.'

I would have liked to volunteer my own views, as someone well-versed in these matters, but I was representing Australia rather than myself. I knew when to keep my mouth shut.

I got to know Sir Percy quite well, not only through the JIC meetings but in the parade of cocktail functions. He was an impressive man, a true mandarin, and a little intimidating: he had a keen mind and was renowned for his cutting remarks. As well as his role as chairman of the JIC, he was Thatcher's policy adviser on international affairs. This dual position was unusual, since there was always the prospect of a conflict between intelligence assessment and policy.

The new director of JIO and therefore my new boss, Dr Paul Dibb, was due to pay a visit to London. He was keen to talk to Sir Percy, whose policy–intelligence combination would be useful for a particularly delicate matter Paul – as he encouraged me to call him – wished to discuss. Sir Percy was also keen to talk to Paul, who was an expert on the politics of the Soviet Union and had recently published a controversial book on the subject. Paul's thesis challenged the conventional wisdom of Western intelligence agencies by arguing that the Soviet Union was not really a superpower. A superpower required more than military might; it required self-sufficiency and a viable economy, he reasoned. Since the Soviet Union had neither, superpower status was not credible.

I decided that the best way to broach a dialogue was an informal function – if there was such a thing among the British elite. I hosted a lunch at the Royal Horseguards Hotel on the Thames

Embankment. Along with Sir Percy, I invited the heads of all the British intelligence agencies, totalling about a dozen. It stretched my entertainment allowance, but I got the hotel to allow me to supply the wine from my well-stocked booze cabinet.

The timing of the visit coincided broadly with two new words in the English vocabulary: *perestroika* and *glasnost*. These were the terms that the general secretary of the Communist Party of the Soviet Union, Mikhail Gorbachev, used shortly after coming into power to indicate the new direction in which the Soviet Union would be heading. They referred to restructuring and openness, but was there really a change, or was this just political posturing?

At the lunch, everyone was hanging on Paul's words. Yes, he said, the Soviet Union was at the beginning of a fundamental and radical change, and the days of the old Soviet Union were limited. On his way to London, he said, he had stopped in Washington, where his views were well received, with the director of the CIA confiding, 'My analysts are asleep.'

I was struck by the UK intelligence heads' seeming acceptance of Paul's views. Their analysts were cynical of Gorbachev's announcement and did not seem to think there would ever be any change in the 'old enemy'. Paul's assessment was received as a breath of fresh air. But I think that even he would have been surprised by how rapidly his prediction came true when, in just two years' time, the Berlin Wall, the barrier between East and West, fell.

After the lunch, Paul asked me, 'Rod, did you notice that we were the only people at the table today whose names did not start with "Sir"?' We both had a chuckle before he added, 'You know, this has been the highlight of my career.'

He explained that as a former Brit from a poor Yorkshire mining town, he could never have had such hold on the 'Sirs' at the table if not for the opportunities Australia had provided. Knowing the British system, at least as it was then, I tended to agree.

I had arranged a private meeting with Sir Percy for the following day to raise Paul's 'delicate matter'. Indonesia was about to purchase Rapier anti-aircraft missiles from the UK government. This was of concern to Australia, because if there was ever a conflict with Indonesia, such as over the Papua New Guinea border, our aircraft would be highly vulnerable to these modern surface-to-air missiles.

We met with Sir Percy in his office. It felt a little like the Blues Brothers appearing before Mother Superior. Sir Percy was sitting behind an imposing teak desk, and he waved for us to sit on two plain and uncomfortable chairs in front of him.

Paul eloquently explained the reason for the audience and asked whether Sir Percy, as Thatcher's adviser and chairman of the JIC, could authorise the release of information on the technical details of the British-made Rapier missiles. If Australia could get hold of the specifications of the electronics package, we could design countermeasures or jamming equipment. If that was too much to ask, would the United Kingdom provide us with the exact model number? Paul reminded Sir Percy of the difficulty the United Kingdom had in countering French Exocet missiles in the Falklands War a decade earlier, and the number of British lives that had been lost because of that.

Sir Percy perambulated around the issue. Then, steepling his fingers and looking over his half-rimmed glasses, he said, rather imperiously, 'Well, we will see what we can do,' thanked us for the interesting discussion and dismissed us, almost with a little wave of his hand. Paul commented afterwards, 'Now I know why I left Britain.' We both knew from the tone of Sir Percy's words that we would get nowhere. Of course, to provide us with such information would have contravened the UK agreement with Indonesia, but were we not 'the Allies'?

That evening, to mark his last night, Paul took me to Simpson's-in-the-Strand, one of London's most famous restaurants. It is part of the Savoy Hotel and, in a sort of contradiction, serves traditional English food in opulent elegance. So we had roast beef and Yorkshire pudding served from a silver-domed carver trolley. For dessert, treacle pudding with custard. As the waiter poured from a silver ladle, Paul noticed a lump in the custard and with joking alarm said, 'That's a lump!' Without missing a beat, the waiter replied, 'Yes, sir, that is a designer lump.'

Paul and I looked at each other and grinned. It summed up our experience of 1980s London perfectly: tradition still endured, and British etiquette could be used to disguise all manner of sins.

CHAPTER 5

WELCOME TO THE CIA

'From the outside, the CIA seems pretty exotic, but from the inside, it's a big, bureaucratic place. Think post office with spies.'

Barry Eisler, former CIA intelligence officer and author

I returned to Australia in late 1989 after three years of parties and liaising. Paul Dibb had moved upwards in the Defence department, and my new boss was Major General John Baker. I immediately liked Baker. He wanted to make JIO's work more relevant to the Defence military calculations, and had decided that a major re-organisation was required. I now had to adapt quickly to a very different environment.

Baker consulted widely, and I found myself caught up in arguments to restructure this way or that. What influence I had I'm not sure, but I finished up heading a large section that was responsible for monitoring science and technology worldwide, with the focus on missiles, space and weapons of mass destruction. Without much ado, or formal process, I gained the impressive new title of Director of Strategic Technology.

With the new structure came a new name: JIO morphed into DIO, the Defence Intelligence Organisation.

The organisation had just about settled into its new moniker when on 2 August 1990 Iraq occupied Kuwait. At first, this was just another remote war to us: of interest, but not something that required the redirection of intelligence resources. But towards the end of 1990, the conflict began to draw more attention. The United Nations warned Iraq to leave Kuwait or face 'serious consequences', and the United States was ramping up its military forces in the area. We all knew that if the United States became involved militarily, so might Australia, and this meant the DIO would be expected to provide intelligence on Iraqi capability.

My newly formed section was only somewhat prepared for what was to come. Over my early years in JIO, I had amassed databases on Iraq's nuclear and chemical weapons capabilities, and the missile team had since complemented this with their own. But the assessments my section had been issuing on Iraq were not sufficiently detailed or definitive to satisfy the Australian Defence Force. It is the nature of intelligence to deal in probabilities, because rarely does any intelligence agency have all the pieces of the jigsaw; the analysts must use their experience and expertise to assess what the missing pieces look like. Our reports would use language such as, 'It is likely that Iraq has developed *X* weapons systems' or 'We do not believe Iraq is capable of *Y*, but the possibility cannot be ruled out'. Understandably, with lives at stake, the ADF wanted to know precisely what kind of missiles might be fired at them, or exactly what chemicals might be in Iraq's arsenal, so that appropriate countermeasures could be taken.

In December, I was thrust into the more senior position of acting director of intelligence analysis. I was now responsible for oversight of all the analysis and assessment in DIO, from the political shenanigans in South Pacific island states to the military conflict in Yugoslavia. But my key focus was on the coming conflict in the Persian Gulf.

Open warfare began with US airstrikes against the Iraqi forces in Kuwait on 17 January 1991, followed by an extensive bombing campaign against targets deep within Iraq. Iraq responded by firing its long-range missiles at targets in Israel and Saudi Arabia. These missiles had conventional high-explosive warheads and caused widespread panic. The question everyone wanted answered was, was there worse to come? Could there be chemical or biological warheads in future attacks?

As anticipated, Australia was drawn into this expanding war. Prime Minister Bob Hawke committed three naval ships to the Gulf, along with other support, such as a medical contingent and a Navy diving team that specialised in clearing explosives, so the demand for timely and accurate intelligence was paramount. DIO established a 24-hour watch office to monitor developments, and in my temporary new role, I found myself working long and odd hours.

One morning, Hawke visited the DIO watch office to be briefed personally on the latest intelligence. My expertise on Iraq's chemical, biological and nuclear capabilities came to the fore. I told him that we knew what type of chemical agents and weapons Iraq had, and what the ADF might expect to face in the Gulf region. As for nuclear weapons, I assured him that Iraq was a decade away, and probably more, from developing a bomb. We had little intelligence on Iraqi biological weapons, and although I thought the threat was low, I believed that it would be prudent for our forces to be prepared. He nodded and seemed satisfied with this. Perhaps if he had learned what I discovered much later, he would have felt differently; but that was for the future.

Others in the watch office briefed Hawke on matters such as Iraq's military strength and the political dimensions of the crisis. A senior air force sergeant followed with an update on the latest military operations.

Even as the sergeant began, I felt sorry for him: I could see Hawke's agitation. The prime minister was shuffling in his seat and looking perturbed.

About five minutes into his talk, the sergeant mentioned that two Iraqi MiG aircraft had somehow managed to enter the north part of the Gulf, but had been shot down before they could travel much further.

Hawke burst out, catching us all by surprise, 'What the hell are you saying? I have three ships in the Gulf and now you're saying they're not safe from attack by Iraq?'

The sergeant was taken aback. Recovering his composure, he explained that the MiGs had been flying very low, and both were taken out as soon as they were detected at the top of the Gulf; neither had come close to our ships.

Hawke was not pacified. 'I've just come from the Office of National Assessments,' he thundered, 'and they told me that my ships were not under threat.'

As the acting director of intelligence analysis, I was wondering whether I should intervene. But I was trained in intelligence, not in soothing angry politicians – especially when the politician is the prime minister. Before I could react, General Baker came to the sergeant's rescue. In his careful, measured way, Baker explained that the Australian ships had not been at risk. The United States had taken out the first Iraqi MiG at the top of the Gulf, and the second one had travelled only a little further before it too was brought down. The United States had allowed the Kuwaiti air force to bring down this second MiG for reasons of pride and morale. Both Iraqi aircraft were being monitored by the United States at all times, and if there had been a danger to any member of the coalition forces, they would have destroyed the MiGs earlier. This seemed to mollify Hawke, and the briefing continued.

I've thought about Hawke's outburst often in the years since. 'His' ships were under orders to patrol in the southern part of the Gulf, and even if they were a target, which seemed unlikely, the MiGs would first have had to evade attack from the powerful US Navy Task Force located towards the northern end of the Gulf. Hawke would have known this. I could only assume the real reason for his outburst was that the Office of National Assessments had not briefed him on the detail, and, since the ONA was part of his own department of Prime Minister and Cabinet, this must have been particularly vexing.

The Gulf War was over a few weeks later, due to the collapse of Iraq's army and the destruction of its air force. The analysts that had been seconded to the watch office returned to their regular jobs, and I was soon to return to mine. As director of strategic technology, I could now direct my team to other matters.

Just as I was thinking that Iraq would slip into the background, in mid-May 1991 I was invited to a meeting in the Department of Foreign Affairs. The United Nations had requested personnel to travel to Iraq as part of an inspection team to monitor the disposal of Iraq's weapons of mass destruction – or at least what was left of them after a massive US bombing campaign. Public servants from various government departments were summoned. I wondered why I had been included: I was an intelligence officer, and this was strictly a policy matter. As I sat down, I saw Dr Peter Dunn, who headed the Protective Chemical Division in Melbourne and who I knew from the Yellow Rain days. We exchanged a glance. He was another unusual addition to the meeting.

The chair explained he was looking for advice on how Australia might contribute to the UN inspection process. Peter volunteered that his laboratory could provide technical advice and perhaps even analysis of samples. I said that DIO might be able to provide some intelligence support, although the sensitivity of the information we had might be a limiting factor. The chair made it clear that he was looking for more direct support. As the meeting drew to a close, he asked Peter and me casually whether we would be willing to go to Iraq on the first chemical inspection. We both now saw why we had been invited. We would become UN weapons inspectors.

'By the way,' the chair added, 'you'll be leaving next week.'

* * *

I was going into the lion's den – Iraq shot spies, or worse. It was nerve-racking. At the same time, it was exciting, and a great opportunity. On and off over the last ten years, I had been working on collecting and analysing intelligence on Iraq's weapons of mass destruction, including its research and production facilities, and here was a rare chance to see how much I had got right with some 'ground truth'.

It was a scramble to get ready for the mission. All we were told was that we would be the first UN team to visit Iraq, and that we were to inspect Iraq's main chemical weapons production facility, Muthanna, in the desert about 100 kilometres northwest of Baghdad. Without any real idea of what might be provided in the way of equipment, self-sufficiency seemed prudent. One of my first actions was to secure a respirator and other protective equipment from army stores in Canberra. Since I had had little training in how to use them, I arranged for a quick update at the army's training centre at Holsworthy, just south of Sydney.

Much of my preparation was studying the intelligence that DIO held on the Muthanna plant. Although I was reasonably familiar with the general nature of the facility, I needed detailed knowledge.

This was not easy, as the site had about 100 buildings scattered over an area of about 25 square kilometres.

I met up with Peter in Melbourne, and we caught the plane to Bahrain on 31 May 1991, less than two months after the official end of the war. We were the only Australians on this first inspection team, and we recognised that it was quite an honour – especially as Peter had been selected by the United Nations to head it. However, we had no idea who else might be assigned or what skills they might possess. With Peter's blessing, I decided to appoint myself the team's intelligence adviser, although, for obvious reasons, I would not officially carry this title.

Bahrain was the staging post for entry into Iraq, and over the next few days other members of the team arrived in a trickle. The experts in chemical warfare defence came from Canada, Sweden, Belgium, Germany, the United Kingdom, France and, for good measure, Iran – there were about twenty in all. Curiously, there were no US participants: perhaps the United States considered it a bit too risky given the recent war and Iraq's unpredictability under Saddam Hussein.

Among this motley crew, there was one face I did recognise. I had met Hamish Killip in London, where he had been a chemical weapons analyst. He was a qualified chemical engineer and had worked for a Zambian mining company before joining the British Army. His service included Northern Ireland, where he had developed keen observational skills. He told me that on his patrols of the streets of Belfast, 'noticing a window that was ajar when ten minutes earlier it had been closed could be the difference between life and death'. Powers of observation are what makes a good intelligence officer, and also a good weapons inspector.

The cobbled-together UN inspection team assembled in the Bahrain Holiday Inn ballroom on the evening of 3 June. It struck me as incongruous that we were meeting to discuss a dangerous mission to war-torn Iraq in a location that carried the words 'holiday' and 'ballroom'. After the usual greetings and introductions, I began with a briefing on Muthanna. This was tricky, because I could not reveal everything I knew for security reasons – some of the information I had was classified as Top Secret. I fudged a little because I felt that a knowledge of the facility was important for safety: the site had been heavily bombed just a couple of months previously, and apart from unexploded munitions, there was certain to be leaking chemicals and unsafe structures.

I sat down, and other members of the team gave briefings according to their speciality. Soon I noticed three men sitting at the back of the room, and for a moment or two wondered if they may be latecomers – though my instincts told me they were not.

At the end of the briefing session, one of them stood up and explained that they were from the American Embassy. The US government was happy to help us if we needed anything. It clicked: these were CIA officers, who had somehow weaselled their way into our meeting. Over the coming year I was to get to know them pretty well.

The United Nations planning for this first mission all seemed a bit ad hoc. At that stage, we did not even know how we were to get from Bahrain to Baghdad. Even the name of the UN inspection authority we were to operate under had not been decided until the very last moment. As we stepped aboard a chartered, ancient Romanian BAC-111 jet bound for Baghdad, we were told that we were now part of the newly formed UN Special Commission on Iraq, UNSCOM for short. As I was to learn later, UN internal politics were driving the rush to get inspectors on the ground in Iraq, and this cobbled-together mission was testimony to that.

The inspection of Muthanna began the next week. It turned out to be a reality check for me. After ten years of studying Muthanna, mainly through high-quality satellite imagery, I believed that I knew the place like the back of my hand. But nothing could have prepared me for the reality of the devastation, the heat and, most of all, the pervasive smell of leaking chemicals.

Almost every building at Muthanna had suffered damage from bombings – some were simply heaps of rubble. The challenge of inspecting these was only too apparent.

However, worse were the storage bunkers, which were awesome in their size and construction. They had been built by an East German company and were like something from the Third Reich. Covering reinforced concrete about 1 metre thick was a layer of 2 metres of earth, which was then covered by another layer of concrete. The Americans had scored direct hits with their smart bombs, reducing most of the bunkers to a morass of twisted reinforced steel and concrete. One 20-tonne door demonstrated the power of the blasts – it had been thrown more than 100 metres from its bunker.

Inside this mess were the remains of hundreds of destroyed, or partly destroyed, bombs and rockets that had been filled with deadly nerve agents or mustard gas. It would be a Herculean task for the teams that followed us to account for all these leaking chemical weapons.

Our job was not made any easier by the Iraqis. They appeared welcoming, and happy to cooperate; no request was too much trouble. But there were indications of a deeper plot.

Outside some of the damaged buildings were small piles of ashes, many smouldering. Pointing to one, I asked, 'What is this?'

The disingenuous reply came quickly. 'You must understand, Dr Barton, that the American aggressors destroyed our power supply. So we lit bits of paper to find our way around inside the buildings in the dark. The piles are paper. The documents we burnt are of no interest to you and your team – just personnel records.'

I poked at the embers. Nothing discernible was left. But in the long grass just a short distance away, I discovered a few half-burnt pages that had obviously been carried away by the heat and the wind. They included specifications of equipment that I assumed were used in the production of poisonous gas. This would be something that later teams could follow up.

As I carefully placed the fragments into my backpack, one of our Iraqi minders came up to me. 'This is not allowed. Give them to me!' he shouted. I simply ignored him.

I also knew from satellite intelligence that the Iraqis were not revealing some critical information. About a kilometre from the chemical plant, something had been buried in the desert. Peter and I drove across the sands to this location – much to the protest of our minders – and I found what I was looking for. Half-buried in the sand was a tanker trailer, with some bushes scattered across the top in an attempt to disguise it. Our chemical detectors alerted us that inside the tanker was deadly mustard gas.

This clearly was not the cooperation we needed from the Iraqis. What else weren't they telling us?

Despite all the hazards and difficulties, in just over a week our team collected the information we needed to plan future, more detailed inspections of Muthanna. On the plane back home, I wondered whether I would ever see Iraq again. Just in case I might return, the UN doctors had given me vials of vaccine as boosters to the precautionary injections I had received before entering Iraq. Only when I reached Sydney airport did it occur to me that it might be a problem that my luggage contained a couple of vials of deactivated anthrax bacteria.

I declared the anthrax, and it caused quite a stir. The customs and quarantine officers inspected the vials and did not know what to do, despite my assurances that this was deactivated anthrax in vaccine form, given to me by the United Nations. Supervisors were called, and I showed them my government-issued passport to no avail.

Weary and keen to leave, I suggested a solution: I would write out an affidavit, certifying what the anthrax vax was for, that it contained deactivated bacteria and that if there were any problems,

I would take personal responsibility. This seemed to satisfy all. An intelligence officer needs to be creative in problem-solving …

Back in Canberra, I was trying to return to normality when General Baker called me into his office. The CIA had been in touch about a clandestine operation they had going in Bahrain, code-named GATEWAY. Ostensibly, GATEWAY was set up to help prepare UN inspection teams entering Iraq, but an undercover objective was to collect intelligence. The intelligence they were seeking was primarily what the inspectors saw at sites housing weapons of mass destruction, but it also included a wide variety of other information, including anything that might assist the United States if hostilities resumed.

The Americans wanted to 'internationalise' GATEWAY to make it more acceptable to the United Nations and, of course, to the inspectors themselves. Already a Brit was attached, and Canada had been invited but had apparently declined to send a representative. Would we oblige?

Baker asked me if we had a suitably qualified person to send, and I started to run through which of my staff might fit the bill when he cut me off: 'I really think you should go.'

Coming from General Baker, this was an offer that could not be refused, but I was also a little embarrassed not to be giving a chance to one of my junior intelligence officers. At the same time, I was eager for another adventure in the world of spies.

As I was about to leave Baker's office, he added, 'Just one thing before you go. Select your replacement.'

I thought for a moment that he might be suggesting a back-up for Bahrain, so that if something unpleasant happened to me, I could be readily replaced. But I realised what he meant was that at the end of my three or four months with GATEWAY, he would be asked by the Americans for a replacement. Since there was no one else in DIO with my background or field experience, the training for that officer had to start immediately.

I soon discovered that the 'Brit' on GATEWAY was my UNSCOM colleague Hamish Killip. Strictly speaking, he wasn't a Brit at all; he was from the Isle of Man, and travelled on a Manx passport. But he seemed very English to me, and he also shared my cynicism about world politics. I looked forward to the assignment.

One problem emerged before I took up my posting. What would my official status in Bahrain be? Unlike the United States and the United Kingdom, Australia did not have representation there, so I could not simply be a 'First Secretary' attached to an embassy, like the other members of GATEWAY. In discussions with the Department of Foreign Affairs, it was decided that for my protection I should travel on a diplomatic passport and carry a letter from the DFAT secretary to indicate that I was on official government business. They seemed to be working on the assumption that, if armed with the letter and a diplomatic passport, I could use my skills as an intelligence officer to somehow weasel my way into Bahrain for a prolonged stay. I suspected that it was going to be difficult – and so it proved.

I arrived back in Manama, Bahrain, in August 1991. It occurred to me that if the shoe was on the other foot and a Bahraini with a diplomatic passport turned up at Sydney airport wanting to stay for three or four months for some ill-defined purpose, he would not have gotten far. However, the Bahraini authorities were a little more understanding and gave me a three-day visa – a good start, at least. Somehow, I would have to turn this three days into three months or more. I made arrangements to see the Bahraini head of immigration the following day.

I met the immigration chief in his office. A stylish young sheikh, he wore a robe and a red headscarf. He asked me in impeccable English, 'What is the purpose of your visit?'

I replied that I was here to support the United Nations.

'No problem,' he said. 'You are a UN official.'

'Well, not actually,' I said. To tell him I was here to work with the CIA might label me a spy, so I shuffled uncomfortably, wondering what to say.

The sheikh spoke about the Australian presence in Bahrain, the trade relationship between the two nations and how much he would like to see an Australian embassy in Bahrain. 'So, is Australia to open an embassy here?'

'Well, no,' I said. I decided that the only way I was going to be allowed to stay was to reveal a little of the truth. I said that I would be working with the Americans at their old embassy, but purposely avoided mention of GATEWAY or the CIA.

I saw the sheikh light up. Perhaps he already knew about the

CIA operation. Much to my relief, he said, 'Dear fellow, why did you not say that in the first place?'

He granted me an indefinite visa.

* * *

GATEWAY was located in the ramshackle US embassy, now abandoned except for a small security detachment of Marines and the CIA GATEWAY staff, which numbered about a dozen.

After brief introductions, I was shown my 'office', a former conference room economically furnished with a single wooden desk and chair. There were no windows, which only added to its stark appearance. Most significantly, though, it was outside the secure area where all the CIA staff were located.

The secure area lay behind a locked door and had been fitted with special equipment to allow top-secret communications with CIA headquarters at Langley. Under US security rules, 'aliens', Hamish and I included, were not allowed entry, and so I was isolated in the outer room. This was not the 'full integration' arrangement the Americans had offered General Baker, and I had no access to classified material. Hamish solved the problem by simply not working there; he found himself an office in the British embassy. I wished I had a similar out.

I soon decided that the only way I would gain access to intelligence reports on Iraq was to worm my way into the British embassy. As it turned out, British intelligence was accommodating, so now and then I was allowed to work in the secure area of the embassy. The rest of the time I cut a solitary figure in the large, windowless room the Americans had given me.

Fortunately, the assignment was not a desk job. We were tasked with collecting information from the UN inspectors as they entered and left Iraq via Bahrain. My liaison experience in London came to the fore: it was obvious to me that if I was going to find out anything, I needed to develop a rapport with the inspectors. Hamish and I booked ourselves rooms at the Holiday Inn, where we knew the inspectors were to be accommodated for a few days while they acclimatised and trained. We would meet the new inspectors as they shuffled into the lobby, tired from their journey and bewildered by the unfamiliar sights and smells of the country. Dressed in casual clothes, and often at the bar with a wine or beer in hand, neither Hamish nor I looked like we worked in intelligence. We usually got on well with the inspectors, whether they were from Moscow or Manila.

For most, this was their first visit. Using the intelligence we could share without giving away top-secret information, we would brief them on the sites they were about to visit. The payoff for us was that we would meet them on return and discuss what they had seen. We explained to the chief inspector of each team that the collection of on-the-ground information was important to us so that we would be better prepared to brief the next team. This argument was a bit thin, and some teams, particularly those headed by Russians or Eastern Europeans, saw through it and wanted little to do with us. After all, we didn't work for the United Nations and were actually scooping up intelligence on behalf of the Americans; we had no legitimate right to the information collected by inspection teams.

In fact, a number of the inspectors from Russia, and other countries for that matter, were also in the intelligence business. We often knew through our sources which inspectors were working for the First Directorate of the KGB (and, after November 1991, its successor organisation, the Federal Security Service), and we assumed they knew who we represented, too. Even though we were all from this rather exclusive club, none of this was acknowledged; we just danced around the subject. In Bahrain, we weren't rivals, since we were here for the same reason: to collect intelligence on Iraq. I was deep in the strange world of spies now.

Despite the challenges, Hamish and I usually got what we were after. The easiest ploy was to sideline one of the inspectors from a friendly country and chat with them in the Holiday Inn bar over a beverage. It was important not to appear too keen to elicit information – just to sound interested in their recent exploits in Iraq. Notetaking was a definite no. A memory for detail is a requirement for all good intelligence officers.

There were also other ways of obtaining information. Sometimes it was simply 'helping' the inspectors with the printing of their negatives. The copies we retained would often net us massive amounts of information. Back then, awareness of computer security was limited; even after the inspectors had 'deleted' all their sensitive material on the computers that GATEWAY had conveniently loaned them, we had programs that could recover at least some of it.

UN inspection teams would come and go at all sorts of odd hours, and when several arrived together, the work was intense. But when there was no team in town, there was little to do, and Hamish and I explored Bahrain.

The Bahraini government was repressive, clamping down on dissidents, and many were imprisoned without trial on a small island in the Gulf. But to the visitor, none of this was readily apparent. To outward appearance, Bahrain was relaxed and friendly, tolerant of other cultures. We met some expatriate Brits who seemed to regard Bahrain as England with 365 days of sun: they even had their own rugby and cricket clubs. We enjoyed the old *souq* (marketplace), with its large Indian community, little restaurants and colourful stalls. Bahrain had few licensed pubs, but foreigners could purchase alcohol at select locations.

We often spent Friday afternoons at 'Sheikh's Beach', with its Australian-imported sand. This beach was closed to the general public, as it formed part of the grounds of one of the Emir's palaces, but the Emir was happy for a few select foreigners to use it one day a week. Occasionally he would stop by to chat with bathers, his magnificent white robes edged with gold trim, and Hamish and I in our Speedos just trying to look manly. He would often tell us about the people he had met and the places he had been. Once he recounted telling a joke to the Queen of England about Jehovah's Witnesses: I wondered whether she was amused. He also revealed how offended he was when he visited Sydney, and Australian quarantine officials sprayed his private jet for insect pests.

Needless to say, working with GATEWAY was anything but routine.

One day, a UN inspection team headed by the mercurial American David Kay visited the Iraqi Petrochemical Company in downtown Baghdad. The United States had been tipped off that there was a hoard of nuclear-related documents hidden in the building.

Sure enough, in the basement the team found four trunks stuffed with documents about a secret nuclear weapons program. But before the inspectors could leave, their Iraqi minders blocked the exit; they would not permit them to depart with the documents. It led to a week-long stand-off.

The enterprising inspectors were not to be foiled, however. They were allowed to use toilets at the back of the building, so they removed a few documents at a time, hidden down the front of their trousers. When their Iraqi minders were having a cigarette break, the documents were hurriedly dumped in the team's ambulance, which was parked at the rear of the building, and then eventually delivered to a waiting UN plane. The pilot later told me that Iraqi ground staff had tried to stop his take-off by setting a fuel truck in his path, but he had managed to steer around it.

I learnt about all this because the smuggled documents were delivered directly to GATEWAY at the Embassy annex for safekeeping until arrangements could be made for their transfer to the International Atomic Energy Agency in Vienna.

Eventually, after pressure from the United Nations, many of the other documents housed in the four trunks also arrived. Now my spacious office at GATEWAY became an asset, as there was plenty of room to sort through the paperwork.

Hamish and I took the lead role on this. The documents were in Arabic, which neither of us could read. But we knew Arabic numerals, and so while waiting for translators to be flown in from the United States, we used the catalogue number at the top of each document to sort them into piles. With help from the one translator on site at the embassy, we tried to make some sense of what was lying on the floor in front of us.

Fortuitously, among the mass of papers we found a single page that became our Rosetta Stone. It was the code to the catalogue: now we knew which documents were key and which referred to more mundane administration matters. We prioritised documents for translation.

When the translators arrived and set to work, we soon received reports that shook us. It was clear from these documents that Iraq had an advanced nuclear weapons program that included everything from mining uranium to enriching it. Western intelligence had completely missed all this prior to the Gulf War, so what the documents showed came as a major revelation.

The document that shook us most was a top-secret progress report from an establishment called Al Atheer. This report, which covered the period up to 30 May 1990, seven months before the Gulf War, described the work that had been done on designing a nuclear weapon. Iraqi scientists had solved a number of problems, such as the design of nuclear initiators, and they were optimistic on other fronts that a solution was near.

Based largely on the Al Atheer progress report, my view became that at the start of the Gulf War, Iraq might have been only a year or two away from making a nuclear bomb. I couldn't help but think of the meeting with Bob Hawke, and how wrong my advice on Iraq's nuclear weapons program had been. I had advised him that Iraq was at least a decade away from nuclear weapons; now, I realised they had been on the brink. Would Australia have even risked war if we had this information in January 1991? It was the kind of speculation that kept me awake at night.

* * *

As 1991 drew to a close, my posting to GATEWAY was due to finish. I had one last trip to Iraq. Based on CIA intelligence, a special UN inspection was organised for sites where it was believed chemical or biological weapons were hidden. So as not to alert the Iraqis about the nature of this mission, it was to be headed by a junior US army major assigned to UN headquarters, Karen. As she had no experience in Iraq, Hamish and I were to provide guidance.

By then, Iraq had hardened its approach to weapons inspectors. It was now actively obstructing inspections or using harassment techniques such as phone calls in the middle of the night, public demonstrations outside the inspectors' hotels and even physical attacks on inspectors by 'outraged citizens' (who were really in the employ of the government). On one mission, Iraqi guards had fired shots over the heads of inspectors. The Iraqi intelligence services also bugged inspectors' hotel rooms and rifled through their suitcases.

Hamish and I were to help plan and run the mission, with Hamish doubling as the operations officer and me as the report coordinator and, secretly, the intelligence officer. Many of the team were selected because they had been to Iraq before: they knew what to expect, and how to handle the aggression we were likely to face. But apart from Karen, Hamish and me, no other team member knew the true nature of the mission, for security reasons.

The head of GATEWAY invited us to a demonstration of a new device known as a digital camera. A senior CIA technical officer showed us this rather bulky camera, and a small suitcase full of electronics by which we could encrypt the information and send it securely down a phone line back to GATEWAY. To demonstrate, he took a photo of Hamish and me, plugged the camera into the suitcase, and plugged the suitcase into the phone line. Five minutes later, a picture was printed out on the fax machine. In 1991, this seemed like magic.

We were asked to take this gear into Iraq to transmit the pictures we took back to GATEWAY so they could analyse them and provide real-time feedback. The technician told us they had thought of everything, including the type of electrical plugs and voltage used in Iraq, so that we could fire up the suitcase readily.

I had doubts. If the Iraqi authorities caught me with this, my head – or worse – would be on the block. I could also see another problem. 'Umm, I have just one question. With the sanctions on Iraq, there are no phone lines from Baghdad to the outside world. How do I dial up Bahrain?'

Incredibly, the technical officer had not thought of this. My opinion of the CIA dropped another notch. Given I had no desire to lug this cumbersome suitcase around in the Iraqi heat, this wonderful pioneer technology remained in Bahrain.

Our first inspection sites were in Iraq's far north, and the United Nations decided that we would travel by helicopter. The German government generously supplied the helicopters, along with its Luftwaffe crew; we just had to direct them where to go. Hamish and I assumed our hotel was bugged by Iraqi intelligence, so this made the briefing difficult. Usually, we would brief the team while wandering through the hotel's gardens or somewhere else in the open, and even then we would be cryptic in our comments. But for the German pilots, we needed maps.

Hamish and I furtively ushered the Germans to a room in the hotel, after advising them of the sensitivity of the mission. Hamish opened the map and, without saying a word, pointed to where we were going: Kirkuk.

'Ah, Kirkuk!' exclaimed the navigator, giving away the destination to any Iraqi who might be listening. Quickly, we held a finger to our lips.

'Ah, don't mention Kirkuk,' the navigator exclaimed, in only slightly softer tones. It was like a 1960s television comedy. Clearly, not everyone was from the world of James Bond.

The next morning, we were up just before dawn to avoid the heat. At the airport, our German helicopter would be waiting to take us to places unspoken – or mainly unspoken. Even the team did not know where we were heading.

As we were waiting on the minibus outside the hotel in the gloomy dawn, Karen commented on how cold it was. Hamish, ever the English gentleman, said he could loan her a pullover. She looked at him curiously. Hamish explained that a pullover was something you 'pulled over' your head to keep your body warm – what the Americans called a 'sweater'.

'No, it's my legs that are cold,' she complained loudly. 'What I really need is a legover.'

Hamish and I tried to keep the juvenile smirks off our faces.

The intelligence on Kirkuk was not productive, but that's the way with leads; not everything bears fruit. Yet at our next location, we hit the jackpot. At a sugar factory in Mosul, we found a warehouse of machinery that had been used for the manufacture of chemical weapons in Muthanna, and had been hidden here to avoid the prying eyes of UN inspectors. Under the UN ceasefire resolution in April, this equipment should have been declared and then destroyed under UN supervision. Iraq grudgingly conceded this when we brought our discovery to light. So some intelligence the CIA held was correct.

During this mission, we went to more than a dozen sites. Sometimes we would surprise sleepy guards, who would immediately raise their AK-47s at us, ready to shoot if we advanced further. There would be a moment of hesitation and uncertainty on both sides until our Iraqi minders, who followed us everywhere, caught up and explained that we were from the United Nations and the guards were to let us pass.

Often when we landed at a new site, I would hang back while the team set off for the inspection. Then, I would play the role of intelligence officer, squeezing in between the pilot and the navigator and directing them to fly around the site while I looked for anything of interest. Sometimes this paid dividends. Once I spotted a metal frame close to a bunker. Later inspection on the ground proved the metal frame was for a Scud missile that could be used to carry biological or chemical warheads. But no missiles were discovered in any of the bunkers.

Inspections can be routine and almost monotonous. In such an environment, the danger is that clues to something important can be overlooked. The real skill of the inspector, as with an intelligence analyst, is to remain focused and try to find anything a little out of place, that doesn't quite fit. For the less-experienced inspectors, this was not always easy.

I remember asking a sub-team leader who had just inspected a small concrete building what he had seen. 'Nothing,' he said. 'The building's empty.'

Well, I asked, what had been in the building, how long had it been empty, and what could it have been equipped for? I sent him and his team back for another look. There were always clues: the amount of dust, the type of electrical fittings, the layout of the plumbing, the size of the entrance doors, overhead gantry cranes, even boltholes on the floor where heavy manufacturing equipment had once been anchored.

One technique we developed was the study of bird droppings. Pigeons somehow seemed to get into many buildings, and their droppings would be all over the floor. If equipment had recently been moved, the pattern of the droppings would produce a reasonably accurate outline of that equipment.

The mundanity was interspersed with moments that were truly heart-stopping. The first came at a bunker at Mansuriyah, close to the Iranian border. It had sustained a direct hit in the US bombing campaign in the 1991 Gulf War. It now looked less like a bunker and more like an extinct volcano, with steep sides of debris leading to a crater at the top. Because of the danger, only our explosives expert – German master sergeant Klaus Kessler, who came complete with a handlebar moustache – and me, as the report coordinator, could inspect such sites.

As we climbed the side of the volcano, Klaus told me in his heavily accented English, 'Dr Barton, this is very, very dangerous. There are live explosives here, and they have been cooking in the sun. Please tread *exactly* where I do.'

In his master's steps I trod. When we reached the top of the volcano, we stared down into the crater. The sides resembled a fruitcake, but instead of raisins and sultanas, there were rocket warheads and assorted detonators sticking out through lumps of concrete and earth. And like cake, it was very crumbly.

The next moment, the earth beneath me collapsed. Slowly, I found myself sliding into the pit below. I became frozen with indecision. Instinct told me to put my hands down to stop my descent, or even try to scramble back up to the top, but either tactic might have set off an explosion. Fortunately, Klaus acted quickly and grabbed my arm, hauling me back before I gathered too much momentum.

Even if I hadn't detonated anything on the way down, I could not imagine how I would ever have climbed up from the bottom. I will always be grateful to Klaus for saving my skin, but at the time, as was the way between professionals of our ilk, I just gave him a nod, which he acknowledged with a small smile. I still have occasional nightmares about that 'volcano'.

The second heart-stopping moment occurred inside a bunker that had not been bombed. We knew there was something odd when our Iraqi minders did not follow us inside. Only Klaus and I went in, and we soon saw the problem. Just inside the first set of doors, before the bunker proper, our torches shone on stacks of mines piled almost as high as the ceiling. We could see they were covered in mud, and Klaus told me he thought they had been recovered from the field and were still armed.

'Just don't touch them,' he said, 'and we'll be safe.'

But as he squeezed past the first column, his backpack got caught. As if in slow motion, the column swayed and tipped. Klaus and I looked at one another, believing that each other's faces were the last sights we would see.

When nothing happened, my first thought was, *Well, at least I won't have to squeeze past that column.*

I had a scare of a different kind at another bunker. Near the entrance I noticed a small chart listing the weapons that the now empty bunker had presumably once contained. I thought it worth recording the list because I knew that Iraq's chemical bombs had certain designators: were those designators, or variants of them, on the list? Had chemical bombs once been in this bunker?

Almost as soon as I began writing, I was surrounded by several Iraqi minders, who started to jostle and push me. One accused me of being a spy for the US government, and for a minute I thought he had information on me or my role at GATEWAY. I protested about the way they were treating me, but they didn't stop.

Luckily, at that moment our interpreter, Samih Abou Faress, returned to the bunker and came to my rescue. Samih was a tall, distinguished Palestinian from East Jerusalem. He had been a university professor until West Bank politics overtook him. He had a certain presence, and I noticed that the Iraqis gave him a grudging respect. He spoke calmly but forcefully, and at least for a few moments the minders looked like ashamed schoolboys. They allowed me to record the data.

The accusation that I was a spy came up many times during my visits to Iraq. I was not the only inspector who had this charge levelled at them. As I learned at 'spy school', keeping a cool head was the best counter in my arsenal; I would simply wave dismissively at the Iraqi minders who accused me. These allegations were no more than a ploy to intimidate. I figured if they really knew who I was, they would have taken direct action and not just yelled at me.

My time as an intelligence officer working with the GATEWAY team came to an end just before Christmas 1991. Since I never entered the secure area of the old US Embassy building, and rarely even saw my CIA co-workers, perhaps it's a stretch to say that I was working *with* the CIA. That opportunity came later. Nevertheless, an apparently grateful head of GATEWAY presented me, along with Hamish, with a little mounted plaque for our 'outstanding service'.

CHAPTER 6

INTO AND OUT OF AFRICA

> 'In countries where innocent people are dying, the leaders are following their blood rather than their brains.'
>
> Nelson Mandela

I returned to my regular job in the DIO in January 1992. After my adventures in Bahrain and Baghdad, the intelligence work in Canberra looked a little ordinary, but I assumed I would soon settle back into the routine.

It was not long, though, before I began to be concerned about my health. I was losing weight, and ill-defined pains racked my body. My doctor put me on painkillers, and the specialists did their usual poking and probing, but no diagnosis could be made. I continued to deteriorate, and by March was admitted to hospital. General Baker was also concerned. We both wondered if it was possible that I had succumbed to some disease in Iraq, perhaps even been exposed to a biological weapon that we had been searching for but not actually found.

Overseas inquiries soon determined that I was the only UN team member with the symptoms. After a lot more poking and probing, a benign tumour was discovered in my spinal cord. The operation to remove it was successful, and I embarked on recovery.

During this recovery period, I went to Adelaide to see family and friends. It was here I met up again with Jan, my former secretary. Some of my London friends had described her as my 'Ms Moneypenny', but she had a style, sophistication and intelligence that belied this patronising label. It was probably these qualities that ASIO saw in her when she was recruited. Being a housewife with four children was a perfect foil for a job with one of Australia's top intelligence agencies. Even her closest friends were unaware of the nature of her work, and if asked she would simply say that she worked for the Attorney-General's Department, deflecting any further interest.

Jan was in the distant outpost of Adelaide possibly to conduct secret undercover work of an unknown nature, or possibly to do something else. However, she was about to return to ASIO headquarters in Canberra. She had recently separated from her husband, and soon sparks flew between us. We formed a closer connection than Bond and Moneypenny: she became my life partner.

It was a bonus that we both belonged to the same club: the Australian intelligence community. Even so, there were times when reticence was the best policy for both of us. The intelligence world is a strange one, and security issues sometimes intrude into personal relationships. We had to draw some invisible boundaries in what we spoke about. But as far as our friends were concerned, we were just Jan and Rod, both of whom seemed to travel quite a bit for work.

After several months, I returned to work part-time. On my first day back, I was about to enter Defence Building L, now with a proud new sign proclaiming it as the home of the Defence Intelligence

Organisation, when I spotted General Baker having his usual nicotine fix. Unusually, he invited me on a short walk.

We strolled far enough away to be out of earshot, then Baker stopped and put his arm on my shoulder. He explained that he had been thinking about the future of the organisation and felt it needed people with real intelligence experience in senior management. 'It's your turn,' he said, somewhat cryptically.

What he was offering – in fact, guaranteeing – was a promotion from Director of Strategic Technology to Director of Intelligence. It was a big step up: my staff would go from 25 to 125.

I wasn't expecting this. Promotions in the public service were competitive, and independent interview panels selected the candidates. On the other hand, all my appointments in JIO and now DIO, from my initial hiring, had been unorthodox. In the world of spies, things were sometimes done differently.

I had a quick think. I had acted at the senior management level for extensive periods, and mostly it did not appeal. It was all 'performance indicators', 'mission statements', 'productivity outcomes' and staffing problems. The job seemed to have very little to do with real intelligence work, which was my passion. I also knew that at that level I would not be permitted to remain very long in the intelligence world; soon they would send me to somewhere else in Defence, perhaps to the Programs and Budgets Division, a prospect I dreaded. To me this was on a par with sliding down into the bottom of a volcano crater of live munitions in Iraq. I diplomatically declined Baker's generous offer.

But the offer made me contemplate whether being the Director of Strategic Technology, as interesting as the work was, would be sufficiently stimulating. I was essentially returning to the type of work I had been engrossed in before my travels to Iraq, and I realised it was time for a change.

As it turned out, I did not have to wait long.

In April 1993, the Department of Foreign Affairs announced it was looking for volunteers to assist the United Nations in another troubled part of the world, Somalia, which was in the grip of a civil war and a devastating famine. Australians had all seen the awful news footage of Somali villagers who seemed no more than walking skeletons – at that time, about 300,000 Somalis were estimated to have starved to death, and millions more were at risk. The United Nations had attempted to provide aid the previous year, but the war prevented much of the aid from reaching its intended targets.

A week later, I received a phone call from the recruitment officer at UN Peacekeeping in New York. They were looking for an expert in disarmament, and my CV showed that I had experience with this in Iraq.

'Well, yes,' I said hesitantly, 'but that related to chemical and biological weapons, not AK-47s.'

The problem, she explained, was that if Somalia was ever to reach peace, a way had to be found to rid the regions of guns. To clinch the deal, she added, 'We think you might be able to help.'

I found it hard to say no to this pitch. The arrangement with DIO was that volunteers would be on special leave while with the

United Nations, so it seemed like the secondment I needed.

One of the advantages of my time in Iraq was that I was ready to go anywhere at a moment's notice. Not only did I have all the survival equipment (sleeping bag, mosquito net, medical kit, folding pliers), but I was immunised against most common diseases and some uncommon ones, such as anthrax and botulinum toxin poisoning. In some ways, I was living up to the Boy Scout motto 'Be Prepared'.

Jan and I had not been together long, but she understood the importance of my work to me and that this was a journey she could not accompany me on. I would fly solo.

The United Nations, however, moved slower than I did. I did not land in Mogadishu until August 1993. It was a shock: everything there seemed chaotic. The country had been riven by a decade of civil war, and only a few buildings in the city remained intact. The impoverished locals scavenged anything they could: schools, hospitals, fire stations had all been looted to obtain wood, piping and wiring that could be sold across the border or used to construct shelters. Even Mogadishu's main power station had been raided, and bits of electrical gear of no perceived value to the looters were scattered along the roads for hundreds of metres past its entrance.

Due to this chaos, all civilian institutions had disintegrated. There were no functioning medical centres, schools, police, courts – and no laws. Someone pointed out to me that there was no crime because without laws there can be no crime. The term 'failed state' was coined for Somalia because there was no government to run anything.

I was taken to my quarters in the southern part of the city, thought to be a little safer than the rest of the town. Security, though, was a relative concept, and the residence I shared with seven other international UN staff showed the rigours of the civil war, pock-marked with bullets and crumbling in parts due to the odd blast from mortars. But it was a traditional Somali house, belonging to one of the richer residents, and therefore had its own fortress style of defence. It was of solid concrete construction and surrounded by a 3-metre-high wall; all the external doors were steel. Our added security was a group of seven or eight Somali guards, all former militiamen, who were armed to the teeth with an assorted collection of weapons, including a heavy machine-gun, which they set up from time to time behind our steel entrance gates, ready to repel any invaders foolish enough to try to burst through.

Despite all this security, no one could seem to keep the rats at bay. On my first night I slept on the floor of my room (it was a couple of weeks before the United Nations provided a real bed) with the rats scurrying around and the occasional one scrambling over me.

As a senior UN employee, I assumed the mantle of head of the household. My first priority was to wage war on the rats. I instructed our Somali staff to identify and block all possible entry points, and then we pursued any rats we could find inside with brooms, bludgeoning them to death. It was a messy process, but over the next few weeks, their numbers dwindled – though not entirely to zero. We had a communal lounge room, and there was one particular chair that we knew had a rat nesting in the padding under the seat; we dubbed it the Rat Chair. None of us would sit in this chair, for obvious reasons, but we always watched with great fascination when any of our visitors would sink into its padded comforts. In Mogadishu, we had to make our own forms of entertainment.

Even with the reduction in rats, some of my housemates were getting the odd bout of food poisoning. As a microbiologist, it fell to me to discover why. The answer was the hygiene practices in our kitchen. We had two cooks, but neither knew much about the culinary arts; they were former militiamen. With some scrubbing and good instruction from the female members of the household, the cooks gradually learned a few basics of hygiene, such as the importance of clean hands and of washing dishes after use. They were given tea towels to dry the dishes, but I realised they had not quite mastered this task when the next evening they delivered our dinner with the tea towels wrapped around their heads, as a way to keep the sweat from their eyes while cooking in our very steamy kitchen. I was never quite sure whether they used the same towels to dry the dishes. I thought it best not to ask.

* * *

As chaotic as Somalia was, the United Nations seemed only slightly better. Staff had been recruited from around the world, and many, including myself, had no experience of the task they had been assigned. The primitive living and working conditions were an added strain, and the constant threat of danger was intimidating for many. A force of UN soldiers from a variety of countries had been recruited for our protection, and in addition the United States had deployed its own military contingent. These forces deterred some attacks against UN personnel, but were still insufficient to make Mogadishu a safe place. And outside Mogadishu and other major urban centres, it was like the Wild West of old.

Shortly after my arrival, the UN created the Disarmament and Demobilisation Division, of which I was appointed the director, a role with the official shorthand of DDD. As grand as this might seem, I was head of nothing: I had no staff, no equipment and no resources. In fact, I had no instructions whatsoever about my duties. I had to find my own way.

However, my experiences in Iraq had prepared me somewhat, and I wasn't fazed. I relished the challenge.

It was clear from the title of my division that the task ahead was to disarm the Somali militias. My problem was how to go about it, and where to begin. Here my intelligence experience kicked in, and I decided that I needed to know more about the militias: who were they, how many were there, what were their motivations? I spoke to many young militiamen and also commissioned a survey, which gave me some answers. I studied the culture of the Somalis and tried to understand the way they saw the world and the conflict in their country.

The first lesson in Somali politics was that everything of importance in the country was clan- or tribe-based. Each clan understood where they were positioned in the broader landscape and who could be counted as friend or foe. About 30 militias were in existence, but there was a constant ebb and flow as various groups merged and then divided. Through the intelligence I collected, I estimated that there were probably 10,000 loyal militiamen, who were highly politically motivated, but their numbers could readily be boosted to five times that by calling on other clan members. The goal of every militia seemed to be to set up a new Somalia with, of course, themselves in charge.

Except for their leaders, almost all the militiamen were young men in their late teens or early twenties. Some, especially the part-timers, were only boys. The youngest I met was only fourteen, and the AK-47 he carried was almost as big as he was. With the anarchy of civil war and the collapse of the education system, the only skill most of them had was how to fire a gun. One Somali elder told me, 'Our young men do not even know how to herd goats.'

If all this seemed daunting, my intelligence told me that scattered throughout Somalia were at least another 10,000 armed young men that I could only describe as bandits. In those desperate times, their main activities were to raid UN convoys to grab whatever they could, as much for survival as anything else. My disarmament task was not going to be easy.

The fighting in Mogadishu centred on the two major clans, rivalling for supremacy in the city. The United Nations, as a foreign body, was under constant attack from one of these militias, while the other gave us guarded support, possibly because they thought this might give them leverage over their rival. Each day I travelled in a convoy guarded by UN soldiers to and from my residence in

South Mogadishu to the UN compound. Almost daily, we would come under some form of attack, from rocks being thrown at us to shots being fired. Once, I was struck through the vehicle window by an angry woman wielding a metal bar. The bruises to my arm took a couple of weeks to heal.

Mortars were also lobbed regularly into the UN compound. One morning, the prefab building I worked in was hit, and several people were injured. But we had become so accustomed to this lifestyle that the rest of us just tidied up the rubble and continued the day as normal.

Having the Somalis take the odd pot shot at us was one thing, but I didn't expect to find the US military training their automatic weapons on us. Yet that is exactly what happened on a couple of occasions. For security reasons we used to take different, and sometimes round-about, routes between our residences and the UN compound. If we were brought up in front of US Army roadblocks, we would be ordered out of our vehicles while American soldiers, aiming their rifles at us, would check our UN credentials nervously.

All this counted as a minor inconvenience compared with the night of 2 October 1993.

Every night was noisy, punctuated by gunfire or a building being blown up, but this was different. It started with a swarm of Apache helicopters flying close to our compound and then, in the distance, the thunder of many loud explosions and gunfire. This seemed to continue spasmodically throughout the night. Something was up.

The next day, I learned what had happened. In an ill-conceived plan, the United States had attempted to capture the leaders of one of the militias. One Black Hawk helicopter had been brought down and, shortly after, another suffered the same fate. The US Army and Special Forces had embarked on a rescue mission, which led to a firefight that killed eighteen Americans and injured about 100. No one really knows how many Somalis died, but later UN estimates suggested it was probably about 1000, with many times that number injured.

The militias dragged two dead American soldiers through the streets of Mogadishu in a display of defiance: they were not going to be defeated by a superior armed force, no matter the cost.

This set of events was later depicted in the 2001 film *Black Hawk Down*, which for many years I could not watch, as it brought back this terrible period. Time, however, dulls the senses, and when I did watch it, apart from its Hollywood burnishing and a few inaccuracies, I felt it portrayed the event reasonably well.

The *Black Hawk Down* episode had a profound effect on the work I was planning. Somali militia opposition to foreign intervention hardened, not only against the United States but also the United Nations itself. My job of disarming the very militias that brought down the US helicopters was now rendered impossible.

Not long after, I had a very difficult meeting with a couple of leading officials from the main rival militias in Mogadishu. It confirmed my view that there could be no reconciliation between the two groups. Change was not going to happen suddenly, and certainly not through the words of a UN official, no matter what incentives I might offer.

Reconciliation had been the first step in my slowly forming disarmament plan. I decided to shift my attention to the regional centre of Baidoa, in the semi-desert about 150 kilometres northwest of Mogadishu. Through the intelligence I was collecting from various Somalis, I discovered there were about six clan-based militias in the Baidoa region, but the violence they perpetrated was not so much among themselves as against the UN convoys bringing food and supplies to the city. These were 'the bandits'. This, I felt, I might be able to handle.

I recruited more staff. 'Recruited' may be too strong; I was assigned two persons from the UN political division, as they did not fit the mould there and were considered troublemakers. But they found their niche in DDD. One was a retired Egyptian general, Mohammad Ismael, a tall, solidly built man with a certain presence who loved smoking Cuban cigars. The other was a former Sudanese ambassador, Abdul Gadir El Sheikh, who had run afoul of his government. El Sheikh was in many ways the opposite of General Mohammad: he was an encyclopaedia of protocol, reminding me a little of C-3PO from *Star Wars*.

I needed more resources to run the division. Simple things like office furniture were my first priority, so I trotted off to an official in the UN supply section that allocates such things. I explained to him that I was head of a new division and to begin with just needed a couple of desks, but might need more later. He surprised me by asking, 'Well, what are you going to give me in return?'

I thought he might be wanting an authorisation docket or some other form of paperwork, so I asked him to elaborate.

Leaning back in his chair, he said, with a sort of world-weariness, 'This is the way it works.' He paused. 'Before I allocate anything, I want to be sure I get something in return. For example, if you were head of IT, I would expect a computer or two in exchange for my desks.'

He was asking for a bribe. I had nothing so tangible as computers or finances, but it did give me an idea. 'Tell you what,' I said, 'I deal with the disarmament of the militias. What I could give you, if I am successful, is peace. This will make your job easier.'

He grimaced slightly, but he could see my resolve, and eventually I got my desks.

This was not to be the last time I came up against corruption in the United Nations.

The additional staff gave me the opportunity to expand my plans for disarmament, and I sent them in opposite directions to gather intelligence on the militias. I needed to know more about what motivated them, and whether they might be willing to join a disarmament scheme if there was some incentive to do so. Mohammad went to the south of Somalia, to the port of Kismayo, where, with his bearing, I assumed he could access senior officials at a moment's notice. El Sheik, I sent to the far north. He surprised me when he reported on his return that to gain access to some of the most dangerous parts of the region, he had disguised himself as a poor Somali, and because he could not speak the language, pretended he was deaf and dumb. This was how he managed to get through the militias' roadblocks. This felt risky; I advised more caution in the future. Nevertheless, I was impressed by his ingenuity.

Both returned with valuable information on the militias in their respective regions. The CIA would have been proud of them, as I was. El Sheik also proved adept at collecting intelligence within Mogadishu, and I found him a fount of information. We struck up a friendship. He became eternally grateful to me when I supplied a pack of cards and showed him how to play various games, such as Patience, which I found him at regularly in his spare time.

One morning, El Sheik came into my office and said, 'Mr Rod, you have to be very careful. A militia group has placed a price on your head.' I had told him to call me by my first name, but his diplomatic training and sense of protocol never permitted him to speak to me without giving me some sort of formal title.

For a moment I wondered which militia, but my main thought was: how much was I worth? An appropriate amount for a bounty might be $100,000, but given this was Somalia, $1000 was probably more accurate.

'How much?' I asked.

'A hundred dollars.'

I felt the twinge of disappointment. Surely I was worth at least double? Still, I figured this was probably an annual income for the average Somali, so I shouldn't complain.

Soon, another person was assigned to my division. Major Francesco Andreani from the Italian army turned up one morning unexpectedly and told me he had been attached to DDD. Andreani was of diminutive stature, and I soon found that he had great observational skills and a keen awareness of potential danger. I suspected he may have been from the Italian military intelligence services, but avoided raising this with him in case my background came to light in the course of the conversation. If it became known that I too was a spy, no doubt my head would be more valuable.

Major Andreani became my shadow, following me everywhere. He was armed only with a small Beretta pistol, which to me looked like a toy gun against the militias' AK-47s. I suspected that he was there for my protection, although I never asked him this directly.

Somalia had once been an Italian colony, and many older Somalis spoke Italian. Andreani would engage them in conversation and pick up useful information from time to time. With him, my little motley network of spies was complete.

My attention was now firmly on Baidoa. I believed that many of the militias there would abandon fighting if they were given an alternative, and my plan was to offer them vocational training. Since the country had been torn asunder by looting, I thought that something along the lines of a woodworking and joinery shop might be useful, so that schools and public buildings could be rebuilt. This would only be a pilot program, and if it was a success, I would look at extending it to similar regions. The intelligence work that Mohammad and El Sheik had done would be useful in this regard, too.

I chose Baidoa not only because the clan politics were not as deeply entrenched as elsewhere, but also because it was an area where the Australian forces, as part of the United Nations, had brought a measure of peace earlier in the year. I thought that as an Australian I might be welcomed by the locals.

I organised a helicopter to Baidoa. The Russians flew their ageing Mil Mi-8 helicopters like a taxi service for the United Nations. Sitting inside an Mi-8 was like sitting in an old minibus, except a lot noisier, and with bone-rattling vibrations. These were not the type of helicopters I was used to flying in with the German Luftwaffe in Iraq! The Russian pilots also flew very close to the ground for 'safety reasons'. I always wondered why. Was it so we could come and go before anyone on the ground had time to grab their gun, or was it in case of engine failure? Either way, it made no sense to me, but I kept quiet about this and instead appreciated the scenery as we skimmed across the desert, occasionally scaring herds of camels and a few local villagers.

My shadow, Major Andreani, accompanied me to Baidoa, and I welcomed his presence on this trip into the unknown. Upon landing we were met by the UN district commissioner, who took us to our accommodation at the 'palace' – ironically, it was once the residence of Siad Barre, the former president of Somalia, who was in large part responsible for the civil war that had devastated the country and led to UN involvement.

The district commissioners were part of the UN political division, and their role was largely to help establish local councils and provide administrative support to other elements of the United Nations. In practice, they often took on the mantle of governor, and this was only reinforced by the fact that their lodgings were usually a palace, or the offices of the former regime. It smacked of colonialism, but that was not my concern now. I needed advice.

I asked the commissioner about the local marketplace. As in many countries, the market is where information is exchanged, and this was particularly true in Somalia. The civil war meant that there were no newspapers and few radio stations. In any case, the only local broadcasts were by militia groups sending out propaganda. A universal Somali written language was only introduced in 1972, and Somali society still had a very oral tradition of passing on news.

My plan was to use the marketplace to introduce myself to the locals. The commissioner advised against this – he had never been through the market himself, as it was considered too dangerous for an outsider to enter. I was insistent, though, and reluctantly he authorised transport – and assigned a carload of armed guards to accompany me.

The last thing I wanted was a group of armed guards walking through the market. This would send totally the wrong message. So, when we were close to the market, I asked to stop the cars and told the guards to stay with the vehicles. I suggested to Major Andreani that he could also stay if he wished, but, ever loyal, he said he would accompany me.

I strolled through the market trying to look casual, but with a knot in my stomach. My spy school training had taught me to appear confident, and one part of me was: I had assessed the situation and believed the risk in Baidoa was not that great. Moreover, the gains would be well worth it. However, one factor I was unsure about was the influence that the recent Black Hawk incident, which took place in the Bakaara Market in Mogadishu, had had on the Baidoa populace.

I turned and saw that Major Andreani, who was following me closely, was clearly nervous. He was looking left to right, clutching the Berretta in his holster. If we were attacked, neither his camouflage uniform nor his little gun would have made much difference; I told him not to worry.

The marketplace was crowded and noisy. Everything from clothing to yams were being traded. One stall had sides of goat hanging in the stifling heat, immersed in clouds of flies. Exotic smells wafted in from stalls selling a variety of spices, most of which I had never seen before. The Somalis in front of us simply parted, staring with curiosity at two white men on a morning stroll.

About ten minutes in, a tall, stocky Somali came and stood in front of me, blocking my path. He was clearly a man of influence, and the crowd went quiet, watching intently for what might follow. He pointed a finger at my chest and said loudly, 'You, American.'

I wasn't sure whether this was an accusation or a question, but replied so that all could hear, 'No, Australian.'

A buzz went through the gathering crowd and I could hear the words, 'Australia! Australia!'

Someone asked, 'Is Australia coming back to Baidoa?'

I said no, and explained that I was with the United Nations and would work with the militias to help rebuild schools and other buildings, if the people wanted it.

At that, the large Somali's face cracked into a wide smile. He shook my hand vigorously and said, 'Welcome to Baidoa.'

He accompanied Andreani and me on the rest of our stroll. I was grateful for this, not only as it showed the locals a level of acceptance, but because as we approached a meat stall further into the market, the stallholder, wielding a machete, approached, shouting something I didn't understand except for the word 'America'. My tall Somali guide yelled something back, and others ushered the man aside.

The walk-through went better than I had expected. Being stopped in the centre of the market had given me the chance to explain to the assembled mass what I was doing in Baidoa and perhaps gain some support for my project. I knew this news would be all over town by sunset, and within a few days, hopefully the militias in the nearby bush too would have heard.

Back at the palace, I asked the district commissioner to help organise two meetings for the next day, one with the elders who ran a newly formed district council, and another with the heads of the militias.

The meeting with the elders was straightforward. My appearance in the marketplace had generated interest. I spoke about the militias in the area, offering my understanding of who they were. I explained that if we could provide some alternative for these young men, they may be induced to give up their weapons. I told them of my ideas for a carpentry program, given there was a need to replace doors, windows, roof trusses and school desks that had been looted.

The council leader, Musse Hussein, an elderly and distinguished man in traditional Somali dress, welcomed the initiative and acknowledged that the militias in the area were causing problems in the town because of their hold-ups and looting. But he pointed out that an aid agency had already begun a carpentry training workshop. What he would really like us to do, he said, was to build a farm on the edge of town and incarcerate the militias on it.

I told the elders that if they wanted a farm, that is what I would try to build. At the same time, I volunteered politely, if the militias were to be reintegrated into society, they needed to live in that society, not be locked up on a farm on the outskirts of town. Eventually Musse accepted this compromise.

Now, somehow, I had to build a farm.

The meeting with the colonels of the militias was not so easily arranged, as they were highly suspicious of outsiders. I had discovered through my intelligence inquiries that the six militia groups represented about 2000 men, scattered within a 100-kilometre radius of Baidoa. Word of my visit had got around and they were willing to talk, but were wary that a meeting might be a trap intended to round up the leadership. They mandated that I meet them alone, and that I be led to the meeting place by one of their own. Now I was wary of a trap, but decided the risk was worthwhile. Major Andreani would have to stay home.

I met my guide at a prearranged place in the city, and we walked through the heat of the early afternoon, zigzagging through narrow backstreets in the fierce equatorial sun. We turned down a small alleyway, chickens scurrying away in front of us, and my guide stopped before a battered wooden door. He gestured for me to enter.

After the blinding light of the street, it took a few seconds for my eyes to adjust to the gloom. Eventually a low table came into focus, around which seven or eight men sat cross-legged on the floor. They did not look about to murder or kidnap me, so I sat down with them. One of the leaders translated for me through our hour-long discussion. The chiefs were interested, but cautious. Eventually they agreed to a meeting with the elders where I would discuss how my ideas could be put into practice. I believed that with the number of successful raids diminishing, they had come to realise that this was an opportunity for a different future.

Getting everyone to agree was only one part of the task facing me. The other was getting the funding and expertise together to establish a farm. This took many trips to Baidoa on the ancient Russian helicopters, but eventually all the pieces began to come together, and construction commenced. One problem that worried me was a source of water. Baidoa is in a semi-arid region, with only the occasional monsoon rain reaching this far inland. I discovered that the Indian army providing security for the area had already found bore water just a few kilometres from my farm site. So my next visit was to see the Indian brigadier in charge, to seek his advice.

I met the brigadier early one afternoon at the Baidoa palace where he lived. He spoke with a plummy English accent, and I learnt that he had trained in England at the elite Royal Military

Academy Sandhurst. He was more than helpful, and introduced me to his engineer, Colonel Sooch, who was confident he could find bore water at the developing farm.

The brigadier also offered to collect and document the weapons the militias were required to surrender to gain access to the farm training program I was setting up. Transparency was a key part of my scheme, so that the militias could see the surrendered guns did not end up in the hands of other militias. Not only would the Indian Army document the weapons and publicly destroy them, he proposed, but each participating militiaman would receive a certificate. This would be used to access the farm program and, as I understood it, also informally in Baidoa as a sort of passport showing their peaceful intent.

Building on our rapport, the brigadier told me that he had few visitors out in this distant province, and would be grateful if I could come for dinner. I told him I would be honoured.

Returning to the palace just before sunset, I was greeted by the brigadier's equerry and ushered to the parade ground at the rear of the palace. This was a large rectangular space of compacted earth, with the palace on one side and the other three sides enclosed by a stone wall. In the centre of the parade ground was a rather lonely open-sided marquee, set up with a dining table dressed in a white cloth. Fine dinnerware for two adorned the table. The brigadier was already seated, but stood to shake my hand and explain that I was about to enjoy the finest Indian cuisine he could muster. But first, a gin and tonic.

True to his word, the food was exquisite – and copious – and so were the gin and tonics. All of this was served by a bevy of attendants in immaculate uniform and white gloves. After a few more drinks (at the brigadier's insistence), I almost had forgotten that we were in the middle of war-ravaged Somalia, surrounded by flat, seemingly endless desert.

About halfway through the meal, the brigadier announced that it was time for the entertainment. The words were barely out of his mouth when two heavy wooden gates in the middle of the stone wall opposite opened, and in marched the Indian Army band, who lined up along the distant wall. For a moment it looked a little like a firing squad, but they carried musical instruments rather than guns. The bandmaster took his place and nodded to start them off on a passable version of 'The Sound of Music'. With not a hill in sight, I couldn't help but think what a bizarre world I had found myself in.

By now, the stars were shining brightly, and the brigadier, with a gin and tonic in hand, said, 'Do you mind if I ask you a question? It's a bit sensitive, so I don't mind if you don't want to answer. But: why was the Australian Army so popular when they were here? I can understand why the French were disliked, but most of my soldiers are peasants like the Somalis, and yet we are not as well favoured as the Australians.'

To buy a bit of time as I struggled to find the words to answer him, I fatuously agreed that no one liked the French, who had followed Australia in controlling this part of Somalia under the UN mandate. The truth was, I had seen the way his soldiers treated the locals, whom they seemed to regard as below them, whereas the Australians had shown respect. I felt I could not tell him this. So I suggested that the favouritism may have had something to do with the fact that when the Australian contingent arrived, people were starving: Baidoa at that time had been called the City of Death. The Australians had provided security to the UN food convoys and so managed to save many Somalis in Baidoa from a sad fate.

The brigadier seemed satisfied with this explanation, and we raised our glasses and drank another toast to peace in Somalia. The rest of the evening, for some reason, remains a little fuzzy in my memory.

The following day, I was invited to another sumptuous meal, this time by the Somali elders. Musse organised a lunch in his own home in honour of our coming to Baidoa. An honour indeed. Major Andreani accompanied me.

Although I was still a little full from the Indian feast of the night before, I accepted the generous helpings of goat and camel on a thick bed of spiced rice. It was served with large glasses of unctuous, strong-tasting camel milk, which, not wanting to offend our hosts, I managed to down, with some difficulty.

As I tackled the mound of food in front of me, trying not to notice the heat and flies in the room, I became perturbed by the noises coming from the low ceiling above me. Seeing my furtive glances upwards, the Somali elder sitting next to me quietly leaned over and put his hand on mine, as if to comfort me. He whispered, while pointing upwards, 'There are rats in the roof. But do not worry, do not worry. Before you arrive, we put snakes up there. They will eat them.'

Just when I thought, and hoped, that the meal was over, the main course was brought out. It was spaghetti with a type of bolognese sauce, perhaps in a nod to Somalia's colonial heritage. The elders were fiercely proud that Somalia was now independent, so the dish was probably planned to make Major Andreani feel at home. We both tucked in – perhaps now with not a great deal of enthusiasm, but thanking our hosts profusely for their generous hospitality. It took me back to my days as the Australian intelligence liaison officer in London, and the diplomacy, and culinary forbearance, that I had drawn on to achieve a goal.

Afterwards, I asked Major Andreani what he thought of the spaghetti. His answer: 'That was not spaghetti! It was the worst I have tasted.' I thanked him, too, for his diplomacy.

* * *

A couple of months later, the Baidoa farm construction was well underway, with assistance from the elders and the Indian Army, and I appointed a local experienced Somali to manage its completion. I could now turn my attention to expanding the disarmament program to other areas. El Sheikh was familiar with northern Somalia, so I discussed with him the details of the intelligence he had gained from his trips to this region. It had once been a British protectorate known as Somaliland, and the locals had decided to declare themselves an independent country, complete with a government and a self-styled president. None of this was internationally recognised; as far as the United Nations was concerned, it was still part of Somalia.

El Sheik told me of a demobilisation camp set up by the new 'government', and I thought it worth a look to see if we could learn anything from it and perhaps even provide assistance. So I invited El Sheikh, but not Andreani this time, to accompany me to the hills of Somaliland, and on to Hargeisa, the declared capital of the region. Here, as it turned out, we were soon to face a different kind of music than Julie Andrews had sung about.

Somewhat to my surprise – even though not much surprised me in Somalia by then – the aircraft the United Nations arranged for me was a Douglas DC-3, of World War II vintage. The South African crew assured me that it had been regularly serviced. But my confidence was not boosted when, shortly into the flight, the right engine streaked oil over the wing. Nothing to worry about, the pilot said.

The journey took about two hours. The pilot told me that he would not be stopping to refuel in Hargeisa; he'd simply put the plane down to drop us off and be on his way. In fact, at Hargeisa we got off the aircraft with the engines still running. We had barely cleared the tail wings when the pilot gunned the engines, spun the plane around and sped along the runway to take off.

The reason for this hasty departure soon became apparent. No sooner had the DC-3 hit the skies than five young Somali men approached, AK-47s clutched to their chests. None would have been more than eighteen.

'Landing tax, ten dollars,' they said.

A crudely painted sign on the dilapidated terminal behind them read *Welcom to Hargheysa Internationale Aerporte.*

The reference to 'internationale' explained it all: the money they were demanding was justified, in their eyes, because we had just entered another country. Although the amount was trivial, I doubted that the revenue would be going to a good cause; to me it was simply extortion. I was more angry than intimidated. El Sheikh and my two Somali staff, who were standing behind me, fumbled for their money. I told them to put it away. Then I took the three or four paces between myself and the gunmen. Two of them raised their guns to my chest. When I was within reach, I leant forward and pushed the barrels to one side. They looked a bit stunned. Perhaps no one had done this before.

Taking advantage of their uncertainty about what to do next, I told the teenagers in my best schoolmaster voice, 'We are UN officials and we are here to help the people in this region. If you want ten dollars, go to the UN office in Hargeisa and ask them. But we are not paying.'

As spy school had taught, confidence is the key to success. The militia boys looked rather dejected, turning away and wandering off back to the tin shed that was in effect the terminal.

Later, I mulled over the incident and contemplated whether my principles were worth the price of my life. After all, I knew I was worth ten times that amount in Mogadishu!

The UN district commissioner picked us up and sympathised

over the airport welcome. The young militiamen often fired on aircraft, he said, and that is why our plane had not stayed; it would fly on to Djibouti, where it would land overnight. As there was no UN military in this region, the airport could not be secured. The situation just had to be endured.

He told me he had already arranged my first meeting in Hargeisa. It would be with the 'president', and it would take place that afternoon.

I met President Egal in his palace and found him affable, with a keen mind and a sense of humour. He had been educated in England, and I discovered we had something in common: we had both been Boy Scouts. I explained to him how I thought the United Nations might be able to help with disarmament in the region, and the discussion was going well until he asked, 'Why do you keep saying "in this region"? This is Somaliland, and you should call it that.'

I offered the UN position, which of course he knew well. Personally, I supported the independence that Somaliland had regained; compared with the rest of Somalia, the province seemed to have some sort of order and a sense of hope for the future. But I did not want to be the first UN official to recognise this self-declared republic to its leader.

Despite President Egal's annoyance at my refusal to back down, he invited me to inspect a demobilisation camp, Mandera, that he had set up near Berbera, and with which he would like UN help.

As I left, I extended my left hand to President Egal, who shook it enthusiastically with his left. The Boy Scout handshake.

Somaliland may have been a more peaceful region than the rest of the country, but the drive to Mandera, which was only about 100 kilometres from Hargeisa, was considered far too dangerous. El Sheikh may have been able to pass off as a deaf and dumb Somali, but there was little chance that I could. We therefore had to take a circuitous route, and chartered an aircraft to fly to the long-abandoned Soviet airbase at Berbera. Here we were met by Egal's waiting officials and whisked back in the direction of Hargeisa, along 20 kilometres of bumpy, dusty roads, to the camp.

The Mandera camp was a sprawl of tents huddled under clumps of trees. It was overcrowded with young former militiamen who seemed to be short of everything from food to shoes. A welcome parade was quickly organised, and from a low platform we watched as about 1000 of these former militiamen marched past, arms swinging high as they chanted some kind of war song. I found it all highly disturbing. Far from gaining new skills to allow their reintegration into Somali society, this group of men were isolated, and the only training they were receiving was military-related. It was not something that I, or the United Nations, could support.

El Sheikh and I got back to Hargeisa just on sunset and made arrangements to leave for Mogadishu the next day. The following morning, as we approached Hargeisa airport in a UN Land-Cruiser, El Sheik pointed out his window and said, 'Mr Rod, look out there!'

On a small hill on the side of the road, not 50 metres from our vehicle, was a line of about a dozen 'technicals'. These were trucks with the cab cut off and rigged with powerful anti-aircraft guns that could swing horizontally a full 360 degrees.

As we drove past, the guns slowly tracked our progress. At this range, if they were fired, there would have been little left of us or the LandCruiser. I had a foreboding that if we actually reached the airport, the teenagers would be there again, demanding a departure tax. Had the militias just upped the ante?

Curiously, at the airport there was no sign of the boys with their guns. Perhaps the technicals were there for a show of power, or simply as a sort of farewell. Either way, on subsequent visits to Hargeisa I saw neither the militia boys nor the technicals again.

* * *

I was pleased with the progress we were making at Baidoa, although I wasn't entirely sure what UN headquarters in New York might think. The Americans didn't seem behind my approach: an official told me that I should just offer each militiaman $100 for his gun and soon the problem of disarmament would be solved. He added, 'What the heck, we'll even fund it.'

I replied: sure, I might collect some guns, but what happens to a militiaman after he has distributed most of the $100 to his extended family? With no skills to fit into society, he is likely to be recruited into another militia or buy bullets for another gun.

I was soon to find out what New York thought. Kofi Annan, head of UN Peacekeeping and so my boss, was due to arrive. In a private meeting in my Mogadishu office, I explained, a little apprehensively, what I had done to foster disarmament in Baidoa and what I was planning. I also told him I had rejected the American offer of cash. I did not know this man, and half-expected him to lecture me on my mistakes, but in his quiet, amiable way, he simply said, 'That sounds very promising. Keep up the good work.'

My meeting with him made me realise that although I had been making up my disarmament plans as I went along, the United Nations had no internal experts who were going to disagree with me. Although my Iraq disarmament experience was not all that relevant to a country like Somalia, it was better than no experience at all, and perhaps that is why I was chosen for the job.

While I had rejected the US buy-back scheme, I desperately needed funding for the farm. I was at a bit of a loss on how to raise this. The UN head office informed me that they would not help financially, despite Annan's praise. In desperation, I went to see Dr Leonard Kapungu, head of the UN political division for Somalia. Kapungu, a Zimbabwean, was a difficult man to read. Volatile by nature, he could be quick to anger over seeming trivialities. So it was with reluctance that I discussed my funding problem with him.

Surprising me, he offered his help. As it happened, he said, he was off to Nairobi the very next day, where he was meeting with European aid agencies looking for projects they could sponsor in Somalia. Would I like to join him? Of course, I jumped at the chance, and met him at Mogadishu airport the following morning.

He had arranged a private Learjet to fly us to Nairobi; no ageing DC-3 leaking oil for him. As we strapped ourselves into comfortable chairs on either side of a coffee table, the only two passengers on board, I could not help wondering how much this trip was costing, and what I could do with such funds to build the disarmament and demobilisation farm.

The meeting with the aid agencies worked: we secured a commitment of $1.5 million. They particularly liked the idea of the disarmament farm and similar projects I was planning, and we discussed earmarking some of the funds for that. I felt that, at least for a while, I would be able to continue my work. But I should have realised nothing is quite so easy. Back in Mogadishu, the money was allocated elsewhere, and I never saw a cent of it.

So I managed, with a bit of wheeling and dealing – all legal, of course – to purchase the materials to build the farm. In this I was helped greatly by various UN agencies, which each contributed what they could, and by March 1994 the farm was nearing operational completion, or at least a rudimentary working condition. Thanks to the Indian Army, along with some itinerant Texas oilmen who happened to have a drill rig in the region, we had bore water. I even sourced some chickens during a trip to Mombasa, Kenya. I could have assigned this task to one of my staff, but I had wanted to visit since my days of exile in the geography classroom at Elizabeth South Primary, where I had first encountered this seemingly magical port with its romantic name. The opportunity was too good to miss.

Now, the first of the former militias would soon be arriving at the farm after surrendering their guns to the Indian Army. They would be taught how to plant crops and look after my Mombasa chickens. I decided that we should have a little official opening ceremony. I invited the local elders and senior militiamen. On the day, I arrived at the farm about an hour before the official start time to check that everything was in order and there were enough seats for the invited guests. My staff, El Sheikh, Mohammad and (of course) Major Andreani, accompanied me.

Just after we arrived, I heard shouting. There was a commotion near the gate. A flatbed truck carrying several Somalis raced up the road towards me. As it pulled to a halt, one of the Somalis yelled at me through the dust, 'Man shot.'

Sure enough, there was not one but two Somalis lying in the tray, in a pool of blood. The first looked to have only a small wound in his right cheek, but then I saw he had been shot in the head, and the rear of his skull was missing. His companion was alive but had a deep wound to his left thigh. He was clearly in shock and bleeding profusely.

I needed to act quickly. Delving into my backpack, I recovered my pocketknife and some duct tape. During my Boy Scout days I had learned a little first aid and knew the man would die without a tourniquet. I cut away his trousers and dug out the only thing I could find in my pack as a pressure pad, a spare pair of underpants, taping them tightly over the wound. It stemmed the bleeding. From his shredded trousers, I recovered his wallet. A bullet had passed cleanly through it, including a stack of Somali notes inside. Before the truck rushed off to the Baidoa hospital, I tucked the wallet back into his other pocket, after adding a $10 note, hoping he would find this later.

I barely had time to wash the blood off my hands before Musse arrived. 'I am so sorry,' he said by way of greeting.

I wondered what the crisis was now. Throughout the convoluted process of building the farm there had been many difficulties, and I dreaded some overwhelming new obstacle.

'I am so sorry,' he repeated. 'Australia is on fire.'

I was still puzzled until he explained that he was referring to bushfires near Sydney, which he had heard about on the BBC World News Service. He added, 'When Australia is on fire, it is like Somalia is on fire.'

I was deeply touched. His comment seemed to me a genuine reflection of the gratitude that he held towards Australia, from the period when the Australian Army came to rescue the 'City of Death'.

Elders, and senior militiamen who felt safe enough to attend, began to arrive. After short speeches from Musse and me, I announced that I would give a demonstration of boomerang throwing. There were puzzled looks all round. I removed the boomerang from my pack and, although I was a little out of practice, threw four near-perfect loops, to the applause of the crowd. Major Andreani asked for a try, but could only seem to throw it into the ground; he was, after all, naturally very close to it. Then it was El Sheikh's turn. He put his whole shoulder into the throw, and it was good except for the direction – it spun into the gathered crowd, almost scything down dignitaries as it went. I thought we had better wrap up quickly before another clan war broke out. I said a few hasty words of farewell and presented the boomerang to Musse.

I knew by then that this would be my last trip to Baidoa, and I would not be in Somalia long enough to see the farm in operation. I had been contemplating my future for some time. Although I enjoyed the work, the violence was wearing me down. I had seen it up close too often. The shooting of the Somalis at the farm earlier that day was just another incident in an endless parade. Even my UN housemates in Mogadishu were not spared. Of the eight of us, a young American had been shot and killed on his way to the UN compound; another, shot in the leg; and a third, wounded in the shoulder by shrapnel from a mortar. My job carried far more risk than any of theirs, and somehow I had been fortunate enough to escape unharmed. I knew that my luck would not last forever.

The farm proved a success. In the first year of its operation, 300 Somalia militiamen from the Baidoa region handed in their weapons and, in return, received training in basic farming techniques. Although it was only small-scale, it showed that even in a country still at war with itself, the principles I had set up for disarmament, demobilisation and reintegration could work. Even after the United Nations pulled out of Somalia a little over a year later, the farm continued to run smoothly for many years under management by the council of Somali elders. I was particularly pleased with this because the US official who had offered money for guns had suggested that if the farm was given to the Somalis, they would rip it apart and run off with everything. Little did he understand Somali pride and culture.

The United Nations has since significantly developed the principles of disarmament, demobilisation and reintegration, and now operates DDR programs in about nine countries, including Somalia.

Although my role in Somalia had taken me far from intelligence work, I had used some of those skills to do the job. It was one of the most rewarding times of my working life. I could see that, even in the most difficult of circumstances, it was possible to have a positive impact on people's lives.

Somalia also brought home to me something that all intelligence officers should be aware of but that is very often overlooked – the importance of understanding the culture of a country. Full appreciation probably takes a lifetime of living in a country, but even being there for a few months gives an insight into the way the people and leadership see the world, which is often very different from our view. It was a lesson that became vital when, later in my intelligence career, I was back working with the CIA.

CHAPTER 7

BUSTING BIOLOGICAL WEAPONS

'A lie is not a lie when you are ordered to lie.'

Dr Rihab Taha

On my return from Mogadishu in April 1994, a friend met me at Sydney airport. As I got into his car, I felt decidedly uncomfortable. And then it hit me: this was the first time in about six months that I had been in a car without at least two guards touting AK-47s. I could see it was going to take a little time to return to ordinary life. I was mentally exhausted by all the killings, hold-ups and corruption of the last few months.

In the lead-up to leaving Mogadishu, I had taken a call from New York. An American, whom I later realised worked with the CIA, had asked me if I wanted to return to the UN operation in Iraq as the head of either the chemical or the biological weapons inspection team. The choice of team was mine, but I needed to leave immediately, as the work was pressing. I told him I was interested in the biological position but I had to tie up loose ends in Somalia, which might take a month or two. Then I needed two months' break back in Australia. He said the job could not be held open, but if there was a vacancy later in the year, I would be considered.

I had barely settled back in as Director of Strategic Technology when a woman from the United Nations called me, offering me the position of head of the biological team in Iraq. I told her I needed time to decompress; I could take up the job in September. She reluctantly agreed. I now had to clear it with General Baker.

The United Nations Special Commission (UNSCOM) was an unusual organisation. All of its inspectors, from the executive chairman to the most junior inspector, were seconded staff paid for by their countries of origin. This was very different from my time in Somalia, when, as an international civil servant, the United Nations paid my wages. If I was to join the commission, DIO would be paying my wage and allowances.

UNSCOM also differed in another way. It reported directly to the UN Security Council president, not the UN secretary-general (who was now Kofi Annan, my former boss). This meant UNSCOM did not quite operate according to normal UN rules.

Fortunately, the Australian government supported this operation and I was granted a six-month secondment for the job, which would be based in New York, with the possibility of extension if required. Little did anyone, myself included, realise that the work would drag on far beyond six months: I did not return to Australia for more than two years.

One of the reasons I wanted the job was to help solve what was essentially an intelligence question. UNSCOM had by now been conducting inspections in Iraq for three years, and although there were still some discrepancies over Iraq's nuclear, chemical and missile programs, it was clear that they had existed, and we more or less knew their extent. On the other hand, Iraq denied ever having a biological weapons program. Their attitude was: nothing to see here. The question I had: was this true?

The intelligence DIO possessed showed little of real note, and even the UNSCOM inspection reports revealed nothing that clearly pointed towards a hidden program. The Security Council now wanted UNSCOM to come up with a definitive result: either root out the existence of a hidden biological weapons program or give Iraq a clean bill of health that would lead to the lifting of sanctions. I would be heading the team that would make this final push, and although no deadline had been given, there was an expectation that six months to a year, at most, would be all it took.

This was one trip Jan could make with me. She applied for special leave from ASIO, packed a trunk with shoes and another with clothes, and was ready in a flash. My own preparation was a bit more utilitarian. Before setting off, the Australian Army thought it would be a good idea to 'kit me out'. I went to the Randwick Barracks in Sydney, where I did a quick tour through the army store, picking out respirators, filters, protective clothing, a sleeping bag, thermal underwear, sunglasses … eventually filling two army trunks with things that I thought might be useful.

The major looking after me said, 'We need to kit you out for New York, too.'

I knew New York could be dangerous, but I wondered what special kit he had in mind. For this we went to David Jones, and since my plane back to Canberra was shortly to leave, I very quickly selected a suit, several shirts, ties and shoes. I simply said to the salesman, I will have this, this and this, and in less than ten minutes everything was decided. The astonished salesman asked, 'How would you like to pay, sir?'

I pointed to the major. 'Please ask him.'

The major quickly produced a credit card. I knew then what it might be like to be an eccentric millionaire.

Jan and I arrived at our hotel in New York at the beginning of September 1994. Our first priority was to find an apartment. In a few days, I would be heading off to Iraq on a re-familiarisation inspection. Since this was a work trip, Jan would not be allowed to come with me, and she needed somewhere more permanent to live during my absence.

I contacted an accommodation broker and told her we needed to close on an apartment the very next day. Early the next morning, she arrived at our hotel in a taxi and told us she had lined up inspections at six apartments in the Manhattan area, close to the UN building. After whisking us to three of these, all of which looked magnificent, we found the one we wanted. It was on the thirty-eighth floor of a modern building, and what decided us was the view – huge windows covering one whole side of the building – to the Empire State Building and the art-deco Chrysler Building. With two spacious balconies (which admittedly felt a bit daunting at that altitude), what could be better?

Samples collected in Laos of what the CIA dubbed Yellow Rain – but was actually dried bee poo – at the Defence Materials Research Laboratories in Melbourne. *(Hugh Crone)*

Me interviewing a Laotian Hmong refugee (left) through an interpreter (centre) in northern Thailand, near the Laos border, in June 1984. *(photographer unknown)*

A chemical weapons production factory, Muthanna, about 140 kilometres northwest of Baghdad, in October 1991. Muthanna, which operated under the guise of a pesticide plant, was one of Iraq's key chemical weapons facilities. *(Rod Barton)*

Me outside the entrance to a destroyed nerve gas laboratory at Muthanna, as part of the United Nations Special Commission on Iraq (UNSCOM), one of the first UN weapons inspection teams to enter Iraq. *(Rod Barton)*

Cylinders of the nerve gas sarin dug from the desert at Muthanna. The plant also produced mustard gas, among other chemical agents. *(Rod Barton)*

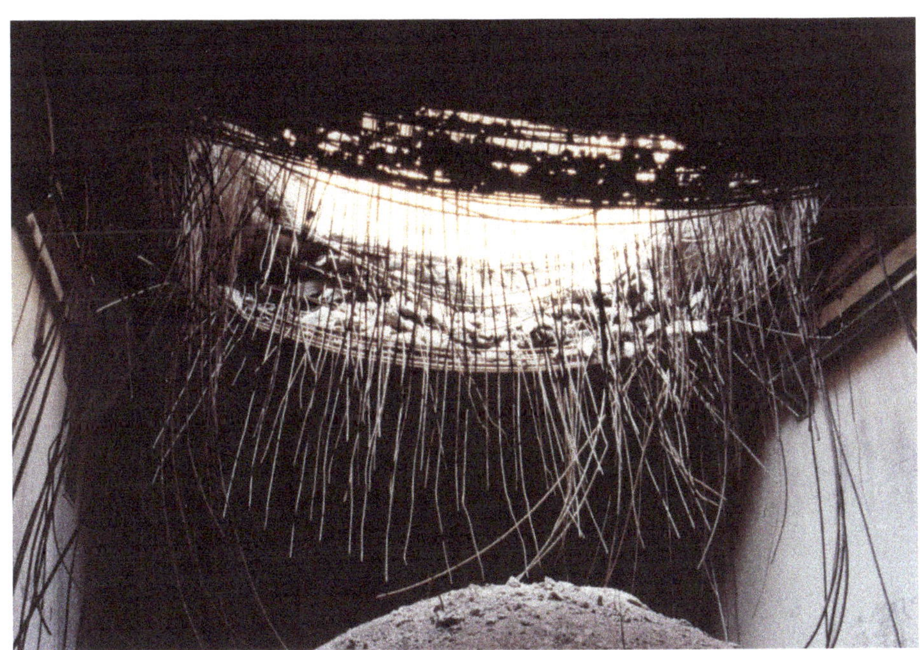

Inside a bomb-damaged storage bunker at Muthanna. The damage to the site had led to the collapse of many buildings, while some remained intact enough to enter. *(Rod Barton)*

UNSCOM inspectors sampling a container of sarin. My colleague Hamish Killip and I discovered about 100 of these containers half-buried along the perimeter fence at Muthanna. *(UN Photo)*

Me with the pilot of this Douglas DC-3 at Mogadishu Airport in 1993, shortly before flying to Hargeisa, the capital of the self-declared state Somaliland, where I met with President Muhammad Egal. *(photographer unknown)*

Militia in a 'technical' – a truck rigged with a powerful heavy machine gun that can swing 360 degrees. I met with several of these in Hargeisa. *(Mowliid Abdi / Reuters)*

Musse, district council leader (next to me, middle), and former militia in front of the chicken house at the disarmament farm in Baidoa, Somalia. In the first year of its operation, 300 local militia surrendered their weapons in return for training in farming techniques. *(photographer unknown)*

UNSCOM inspectors installing monitoring cameras beside a production fermenter at Al Hakam – one of the largest biological weapons production facilities in Iraq, used to produce anthrax from 1988 to 1991. The plant was destroyed under UNSCOM supervision in 1996. (*Rick Maiman / Contributor / Getty*)

Me at the British company Oxoid in late 1994, seeking out the records of bacterial growth media sold to Iraq. These are drums of a yeast extract of the type Iraq purchased for the production of anthrax. *(photographer unknown)*

Dr Rihab Taha, head of Iraq's biological weapons program between 1985 and 1991. The British-educated Taha was dubbed 'Dr Germ' by the media following her arrest. (*Hamish Killip*)

General Amer Mohammad Rashid at a press conference on 7 July 1998. As minister for oil, Rashid held one of the most powerful political positions in Iraq. He was sometimes referred to as 'Missile Man' due to his expertise with weapons systems. (*Faleh Kheiber / Reuters*)

With my friend David Kelly, a world authority on biological warfare and a former head of the UK Defence Microbiology Division at Porton Down, in Baghdad in 1995. (*Hamish Killip*)

On the banks of the Euphrates, Western Asia's longest river, soaking up the Iraqi sun. (*photographer unknown*)

That afternoon, we visited a furniture rental warehouse on Third Avenue. I told the salesman the size of our allowance, courtesy of the Australian taxpayer, and with him trotting behind us adding up costs, in less than thirty minutes we had ordered enough furniture, rugs and lamps to fill our spacious two-bedroom apartment. I was a little worried that the large dining table we had chosen would not fit inside the lift to our apartment in the sky. The salesman looked at me condescendingly and said, 'Sir, this is New York. The furniture is designed so that it can be disassembled to fit in an elevator.' He guaranteed that everything would be delivered the next day, and so it was. It all seemed so surreal.

I could now focus on the coming inspection and get to know the working arrangements in UNSCOM. I discovered that the 'arrangements' were a bit haphazard. The executive chairman, Rolf Ekéus, a former Swedish diplomat, told me that it was a 'collegiate process' – there were no bosses except himself and his deputy, an American called Charles A. Duelfer, on loan from the State Department.

On the floor below the executive chairman, packed in like sardines, were the inspectors, preparing for trips to Baghdad or analysing incoming reports. As I squeezed myself between desks, asking a few questions as I went, one Frenchman, an imagery analyst, seemed to confirm what Rolf had explained to me. 'It is blurb management,' he said.

I thought he was referring to management by rumour mongering, but it turned out his English was good but his accent was not;

he actually meant 'blob management', a concept that I hadn't learnt about during my management training in DIO.

'Blurb management,' he elaborated, outlining a shape with his hands, 'involves a centre, Ekéus, and round him a "blurb". The closer to the centre, the more influence. When the centre moves, the "blurb" moves.' And he slid his hands across the desk to illustrate the concept. I pretended I understood what he was on about.

I was just beginning to think the whole operation was some kind of deliberate chaos when a short, stocky man came up to me and, without saying so directly, made it clear that he was in charge of the biological weapons unit, which was made up of himself and just two others. This person was Dr Dick Spertzel, a retired US Army colonel and a veterinarian by profession. His reputation preceded him: one of my GATEWAY colleagues had given me a heads-up that he was a cantankerous bugger, obstinate and argumentative. Over time I would become used to his ways and we would develop a mutual respect, but on my first day it was a bit daunting. It also left me wondering about the offer I had received to head this unit, but I thought it prudent not to challenge Dick straightaway.

A few days later, I was off on a plane to Bahrain, where I was met by the GATEWAY team. I knew the Australian representative, who was from my DIO group in Canberra, but the others were new to me. The shoe was now on the other foot. It was rather strange to be a GATEWAY 'target', as my official role was now an inspector with the United Nations. At least I was aware of this entanglement and could choose to keep my distance.

Over the next day or two, the rest of the team arrived from various countries, and after the usual briefings and acclimatisation, we departed for Baghdad a few days later.

On this inspection trip, we were to visit thirty-four sites, from university laboratories to a milk-powder factory. All these sites had facilities that could theoretically support a biological weapons program, although none looked to me likely candidates. But the difficulty in identifying a biological weapons facility is that the equipment to make biological agents is often dual-purpose. As I had learned many years ago at the Commonwealth Serum Laboratories in Melbourne, a vaccine plant can just as easily make anthrax as it can a vaccine.

One facility I was intrigued by was what the Iraqis described as a single-cell protein production factory – essentially a plant manufacturing a type of yeast for animal feed. Al Hakam was out in the desert, 100 kilometres west of Baghdad. It was headed by Dr Rihab Taha, a woman in her mid-thirties who had been educated at the University of East Anglia in the United Kingdom.

I had met Dr Taha a few years earlier, when I was still at GATEWAY. At that time Iraq had acknowledged that, prior to the 1991 Gulf War, it had had a 'defensive' biological warfare program, much like many other countries. Australia, for example, had a 'defensive' biological program run by the Melbourne-based Defence Research Material Laboratories, which I had visited many times. Interestingly, Iraq, after some pushing, had disclosed that Dr Taha had been the head of its defensive biological warfare program.

Now she had allegedly moved on and was head of the relatively new civilian establishment of Al Hakam.

I was eager to see how her facility was faring, and if there were any connections between her past and present responsibilities. Our first stop was her office, just a short drive from the entrance to the facility, where she greeted us with a sort of embarrassed and resigned smile. I had not seen her for two and a half years, but she had changed little – perhaps her face was a touch wearier and her short hair a little greyer. She looked out of place in the surroundings, dressed in an orange floral blouse, a calf-length black skirt and clunky brown shoes.

I was particularly interested in the production area at Al Hakam, because if there were any connections to a biological warfare program, this was where the agent would be made. The site was vast, but with very few structures. As the production plant was 3 kilometres from Taha's office, we drove there, with her following behind in her old green Mercedes.

On arrival we saw a few sheds, one of which housed fermenters of the kind that could make vaccines, wine or possibly anthrax. In this facility, though, Iraq declared that its sole purpose was to make a type of yeast suitable for animal feed.

I turned to Dr Taha and asked how production was going. She was evasive, and started talking about quality control and problems with getting the right strain of yeast. My question was redundant, really, since I already knew the answer from earlier UNSCOM inspection reports. Dr Taha had in fact been unable to produce any significant quantities of yeast. At Al Hakam they kept twenty or thirty chickens as experimental animals, and all would have starved to death if they had to rely on the feed produced in these fermenters.

We drove another 2 kilometres back in the rough direction of Dr Taha's office, to a larger, recently constructed production facility that was not yet finished inside. Dr Taha explained that this building and some others like it would eventually house much bigger fermenters, a scale-up of what we had just seen. Apparently, her lack of success on a small scale over the past six years had not deterred Iraq from investing in a large production plant. I asked Dr Taha about this, and she coyly responded with, 'A child has to learn to walk before it runs.' A strange response, I thought, since they had not yet learned to walk.

The team and I inspected a number of other buildings and even bunkers on the rest of the site, and it was evident to us all that Al Hakam was an odd sort of place. It was clearly a candidate for a biological agent production facility: its design, layout and equipment were all a little strange for its stated purpose, and given Dr Taha's background, it raised deep suspicions that all was not right. Suspicions, though, were not going to cut it with the UN Security Council. If Al Hakam had been used for, or was being used for, making biological agents, then proof was needed. It was the sort of intelligence challenge that I liked best.

Back in New York a few weeks later, scruffy and tired after the rigours of Iraq and the homebound journey, I arrived at my apartment tower with key in hand, and walked past the concierge to the elevators.

'Excuse me, sir,' the concierge said, rising to quickly block my path. 'Can I help you?'

He did not recognise me, and no sort of explanation would persuade him to let this scruffy-looking fellow in. He knew that the apartment I claimed as mine was occupied by an attractive, well-dressed Australian woman, and there was no way he would let me in without her permission. Jan eventually answered the security intercom and allowed me up, to the concierge's profuse chagrin.

The following day, back at UN headquarters, Rolf Ekéus called a meeting with the biological team to discuss our progress. We met in UNSCOM's windowless, secure room, which we affectionately called The Bunker. The atmosphere was tense. I could tell there had already been some discussions during my absence.

Rolf was due to meet with Tariq Aziz, Iraq's deputy prime minister, the man theoretically second-in-command to Saddam Hussein (who had claimed the titles of both president and prime minister). Aziz was of course keen to have UNSCOM finish its work so that sanctions could be lifted. He had been lobbying Security Council members hard, and his visit would coincide with a meeting of the UN Sanctions Committee in November 1994, in a month's time. Pressure was on the team to find the answer to the Iraqi biological weapons riddle.

What made matters more complex was that not all the members of the biological weapons unit thought there was anything to investigate. Opinions were divided over whether Iraq had a biological weapons program or not. Dick became quite agitated, since he was a true believer, and in his blustering way presented scraps of information and theories as to what Iraq's program might look like. He argued that we needed more time to investigate.

Rolf was not convinced and added, somewhat rhetorically, 'What makes you think that after all these years of inspections, you'll find any evidence now?'

As an intelligence officer, my thought was that, if Iraq did have a hidden biological weapons program, there must be evidence somewhere. Perhaps we hadn't been looking in the right places.

Rolf decided to give us a last chance to uncover a possible program. The implication was 'put up or shut up'. He gave us no timeframe, but it was clear we had to move quickly: the Security Council's patience was running out. Russia, in particular, wanted UNSCOM to finish its work so that sanctions on Iraq could be lifted; the Russian ambassador had complained to Rolf several times about this. Apparently, Iraq owed Russia many billions of dollars for the purchase of military hardware and weapons such as aircraft, tanks and missiles. Iraq had defaulted on the payment schedule and would not be able to resume payments until sanctions were lifted.

The pressure was on Dick and me to achieve something, and soon. I had some ideas about how to proceed. A few countries had provided us with fragments of intelligence. The Israeli Military Intelligence Service, Aman, had given us some data on foreign suppliers of materials to Iraq. Whether this was connected to a biological weapons program was another question, but it provided potential leads. I decided we should invite Aman officers to New York to discuss the matter with us. Perhaps they could give us further intelligence.

During Tariq Aziz's visit to New York, Rolf followed up on a request from Dick and me. He told Aziz that the process of finalising the biological weapons issue might be hastened if we could interview the scientists involved in Iraq's former 'defensive' biological weapons program; after all, if the program was entirely innocent, there could be no objection to this. In the past, Iraq had resisted this approach, even claiming that the individuals (apart from Dr Taha) might be hard to locate, as some were now in other jobs, such as driving taxis. But Aziz, with Iraq under pressure from the sanctions, agreed somewhat reluctantly to Rolf's suggestion.

Interviewing the scientists would be a chance to see who was involved in Iraq's former biological program and in what capacity. We did not expect any great revelations but, if it was not as benign as claimed, someone might accidentally let something slip, or at least provide us with a new lead.

Once Iraq consented to the interviews, Dick wanted to plunge in headlong. I agreed we should start soon, before the Iraqis changed their minds, but my concern was that Dick's blustering, aggressive approach would be counterproductive. Diplomacy was a skill he seemed to lack.

'Dick, this might be a heck of lot of work for just the two of us. What do you think about asking some others to join us to share the load?'

His answer was immediate: 'No! Absolutely not. It will just delay things. Time is of the essence. I don't mind hard work, and nor should you. Anyway, I'm already arranging for us to leave in two days' time.'

The more I pushed, the angrier he got, and by that afternoon he seemed ready to explode.

I trudged back to my apartment in a depressed state. My experience as a liaison officer in London had taught me that careful planning and subtlety were more likely to achieve results than slamming a fist on the table and demanding answers. Dick's bull-at-the-gate approach might destroy one of the best opportunities we had for progress in solving the biological weapons conundrum.

Over a glass or two of wine that evening, Jan said, 'Why don't you just ignore Dick – who does he think he is?' And, after a moment's thought: 'Why not just ask Hamish? You have as much right as Dick does. From what you tell me, Hamish is one of the most experienced inspectors you have. And though I've only met him once, I imagine he would be excellent at grilling the Iraqis.'

This made good sense. Hamish's intelligence training would be ideal for this mission, and I knew that if asked he would join us at a hat drop. His chemical engineering background would be just what we needed when it came to questions on equipment and production techniques. And as a former military engineer, he had a profound knowledge of weapons systems: if we were to find biological bombs or rockets, his expertise would be invaluable.

It was also obvious to me that Dr David Kelly, the most senior and experienced inspector we had at the UN, should accompany us on this mission. He had headed UN inspection teams to Iraq a number of times. I knew him from my stint at GATEWAY. I liked David and I knew that he was someone with whom I could work well. And, with his calm, rational manner, he would be a good counter to Dick's erratic outbursts. He would also bring with him a sharp analytical mind and a vast knowledge of the science of biological warfare: by profession he was a microbiologist, and had been a lecturer at Oxford before becoming a lead scientist at Britain's biological and chemical defence research centre at Porton Down.

Early next morning, I told Dick bluntly, 'I'm going to invite Hamish and David to join us on this mission.' And then, to be a little more conciliatory, I added, 'I think they might be useful.'

I expected the usual histrionics, but Dick just said, 'Okay. I'll put the requests to the British government. If approved, they can meet us in Bahrain.'

Either Dick could see my determination or he'd had a chance to cool down and recognised that the added experience might, after all, be 'useful'.

I was pleased that now we had a balanced team that could bring the best to the investigation. As it turned out, we worked together as a team for the next few years – although not without a few arguments. But on one thing, we were all united: we were dedicated to uncovering Iraq's hidden biological weapons program. We became known within the United Nations as the Gang of Four.

Dick would head this mission. He proved great at putting teams together, partly because with his bellicose and bullying ways he could obtain UN resources that other team leaders failed to acquire. I also came to realise that he had an almost photographic memory. Remarkably, he could remember serial numbers on machinery, and had a precise recall for dates. This would be valuable if the Iraqis started to change their stories under duress.

As for me, I trusted that my intelligence background was going to be useful. Also, in my Australia Group days I had learned a lot about the black market trade of goods. I knew about letters of credit (the promissory notes that banks pay out on delivery of the goods), bills of lading (documents issued by carriers to note the receipt of cargo) and end-user certificates (paperwork to certify that the buyer will not transfer purchased goods to a third party). So I believed I would have a good idea of where to look for evidence of illegal or suspicious supplies of materials and equipment to Iraq.

Our little team arrived in Bahrain early in November 1994. Before moving on to Baghdad, we visited the GATEWAY headquarters. Iraq had told us that only ten individuals were involved in their defensive biological weapons program, including Dr Taha. We had a week in Iraq and we believed that we could probably interview about thirty individuals in that time, so now we had to decide who the remaining twenty should be. The CIA would be able to provide us with persons of interest.

The CIA came up with a list of about forty names, none of which we had previously heard. Even the CIA admitted they didn't know what role, if any, these individuals might have played. In addition to these, all four of us had in mind others we had met during our previous inspections in Iraq, those whose skills might have been useful in any biological weapons program. Eventually we settled on a list of thirty-five interviewees, including a few wild cards from the CIA list. They could have been car salesmen or key microbiologists; none of us knew.

The next day, we entered Baghdad, and the Iraqis immediately threw up the first obstacles. We wanted to conduct the interviews at the local UNSCOM headquarters, but the Iraqis claimed this would be too intimidating for the interviewees and insisted that interviews be done in one of their government offices. They also insisted that each person interviewed be accompanied by Iraqi 'observers', who would be able to offer a correction to the interviewee's account if he or she made a mistake.

Eventually a compromise was reached: the interviews would be conducted on 'neutral' territory, and the observers would be limited to three and would only be there to observe, not to intervene. None of this was satisfactory, but it was either this or nothing, so we decided to make the best of it.

Of course, in Iraq, there was no such thing as neutral territory – Saddam Hussein controlled everything that went on in the country. The site that was finally agreed on was a small conference room in the Rashid International Hotel. I had been there before and I knew that at the main entrance was a large mosaic of a snarling George H. Bush with the words 'Bush is criminal' gracing the border. Having to walk across the face of the US president to enter the hotel did not bother us, but we understood that this face-stamping was a great insult in the Arab world.

After the hassle of getting this far, we finally sat down at a table in a small conference room. On one side was the interviewee, with an Iraqi observer to his left and two to his right, one of whom turned out to be Dr Taha. Across the table sat the four of us, plus a UN interpreter.

We had agreed that David would lead the questioning of the scientists, starting with the most junior and working his way up, until we put Dr Taha herself before the panel. David proceeded in a careful, methodical fashion. At times, progress seemed excruciatingly slow, but it was essential to build up layers of background before coming to the pertinent questions. It was the type of questioning that a detective might conduct in the investigation of a crime, and its purpose was to establish a base that left little wriggle room for later inventions. For example, it would be difficult for Iraq to claim that they had not conducted a certain type of experiment due to a lack of equipment if we had already established that such equipment was there and fully functional.

On the first day, we interviewed eight of the ten scientists on the list. On the face of it, we learned little: according to the testimony, no one knew who worked in the next laboratory, no one had discussed his or her work with anyone else (and hence could not comment on others' work) and no one had kept notes. These stories could not be true. No scientist works in a vacuum, and it was inconceivable that none of them knew what the others were doing, especially since their work had a common purpose – allegedly, research into defence against biological agents. They had obviously been well coached, and for the first time I started to believe that Iraq really had something to hide. Otherwise, why not be more forthcoming?

The following morning, we were back in the Rashid early. We had decided overnight to change tack and interview a couple of the wild cards selected from the CIA list, even though we had no idea who they were or what part they may have played, if any.

The first interviewee was Adel Nafi Salman. David asked him, 'You worked for Dr Taha?'

'No.'

David looked a little puzzled. Who was this person? 'Where did you work, then?'

'The Ministry of Trade.'

Turning to me, David said, 'My colleague, Mr Barton, has some questions for you.'

The mention of my name shook me out of my sleepy state; it had been a late night. The reference to trade soon woke me further, as I knew that if Iraq did have a biological weapons program, it would have needed to import a whole range of specialist items that were not readily available in Iraq.

It turned out that Salman had been the chief purchasing clerk for the Technical and Scientific Materials Import Division (TSMID). He said the main items he acquired were electronic components, but also some 'chemical' equipment and materials. Since he was not a scientist, he could not give us details. He did, however, acknowledge that some of this material would have gone to Dr Taha's biological defence unit, although he claimed he did not know her or what her work involved. I then introduced him to Dr Taha, who was sitting next to him.

Salman seemed to me quite a genuine person, and although he may have been coached on what to say, he appeared forthcoming. I tended to accept his account on this point. I was less certain on his answer to my next question. 'Can you provide us with the records of imported items?'

His demeanour changed, and he looked nervously at the Iraq 'observers' on either side of him before responding that all the documents had been destroyed, under instruction. This line had come up frequently. So far, we had been stonewalled on all our requests for documentation.

The other wild card, Ahmed Khudayyer, also turned out to be connected with TSMID – in fact, he had been its director. He confirmed what Salman told us, that TSMID was a special division for foreign purchases for government projects. This was a valuable piece of intelligence, and I knew that I would be talking to these two gentlemen again at some later date.

The interviews with the others on our list ground on over the next few days, but we could elicit no further useful information. We had planned a whole day of questioning for Dr Taha. We asked how she had been selected for the defensive biological program, what the objectives were, how far the program had got and even why it was – allegedly – abandoned at the start of the Gulf War. Her answers were convoluted and at times nonsensical, but David was persistent. Eventually it got to a point where I found her stories difficult to disentangle, and it was clear that David too was having trouble making any sense of anything she said. Finally, he had enough, and said quietly but purposefully, 'Dr Taha, please stop!'

I recall her trying to pick up a glass of water, but her hand was shaking so much, the water spilled. She stood up and tried to speak, but no words came. Then, to the astonishment of all of us, she simply burst into tears and fled from the room.

Dr Taha's somewhat bewildering behaviour concluded the interviews, and the next day we left Baghdad. Dick and I briefed Rolf Ekéus back in New York. True, we had not uncovered any hard evidence, but we were now sure that Iraq was hiding something. We discussed how Dr Taha's evasiveness might be interpreted. I also told Rolf that we had some new leads to follow up with the TSMID officials. Rolf, under pressure to wind matters up, was not convinced by our arguments, but he acknowledged that there were some loose ends that needed to be resolved. And with Aman intelligence officials from Israel due to talk to us in just over a month's time, he was willing to give us some leeway – for now.

Two Israeli military intelligence officers arrived at our UN offices at the beginning of January 1995. Somehow, someone had also organised a visit from senior Iraqi officials for the same day – the last thing we wanted was for them to bump into our other guests in the corridor. Dick and I were required to be at the meeting with the Iraqis that morning, so embarrassingly I had to ask one of our UN support staff to usher the Israelis down to the cafeteria on the first floor, where we would meet them at lunchtime for preliminary discussions in a quiet corner. Even this turned out to be unsatisfactory, as shortly after sitting down with them, I spotted some members of the Iraqi delegation entering at the far side.

We decided that the safest place was my apartment, just a short walk from the UN building. I thought to call Jan first so she could be prepared for the visitors.

I had met with agents from Aman and Mossad (Israel's foreign intelligence agency) on a couple of intelligence exchanges in DIO in Canberra, and I respected their professionalism and objectivity. Although I had never met the two agents we had invited to New York, I think they somehow understood I was in the same business as theirs, and we had an immediate rapport. The meeting in my apartment was not going to be an information exchange, since anything we had garnered from our inspections in Iraq was strictly confidential to the United Nations. Nevertheless, I sensed the two officials would be forthcoming.

Jan had coffee and biscuits ready and then discreetly retired to another room; her ASIO training meant she was familiar with the procedure. We were a little nest of spies trying to find chinks in the Iraq armour to uncover its biological weapons program, sitting down to discuss business on my rented chairs, around my rented coffee table, with views of the New York skyline in the expansive windows of my rented thirty-eighth-floor apartment. I couldn't help but think how bizarre this setting was for such a serious topic.

The two Israeli agents read from their notebooks. No documents could exchange hands, so Dick and I frantically scribbled notes, interrupting now and then to verify details, while downing coffee and wiping away crumbs from the occasional Tim Tam. They provided us with an incredible wealth of information, mainly on imports to Iraq over the past ten years. I did not ask for their sources, but as an intelligence officer I had a reasonable idea where most of it had come from, and also had a reasonable idea that most of it would be correct.

What I struggled with was how much of this, if any, was relevant. It was the typical intelligence analyst's dilemma. For example, a laboratory incubator imported to Iraq could equally be for a university research laboratory as for a biological weapons program. Rarely did the Israelis have details on what company was importing the item or the item's final destination in Iraq. But information is always important, as it may connect with other relevant information.

The connection came about with a passing reference to an Iraqi agency they knew only as TSMID. It immediately sparked visions of my interviews with the two gentlemen just over a month earlier. They had told me that some of the items TSMID purchased went to Dr Taha's unit. My interest was heightened – anything purchased by TSMID was potentially for a weapons program. What was TSMID importing?

The Israelis said that, according to their information, TSMID had bought several tonnes of bacterial growth media from a British company, Oxoid, a subsidiary of Unilever. Growth media are nutrients, such as casein protein extracted from milk, that are mixed with water to allow bacteria to multiply in a fermenter. There are many legitimate uses for this material – for example, in the production of vaccines or antibiotics – but Iraq did not have such industries, at least not on the scale requiring tonnes. And why was it being imported by TSMID and not the vaccine plant itself? Iraq had some questions to answer.

The investigation of Iraq's importation of bacterial growth media was a job that I was well qualified for, and I started immediately. What I wanted to know was how much media Oxoid had sold to Iraq, and what types. I was also interested in any other inquiries that Iraq may have made to Oxoid, because this might lead us to other suppliers. I thought the best way to investigate was to visit the company directly, as this was the sort of information no formal request was likely to yield. I wrote a letter to the British ambassador to the United Nations, asking for the UK government's approval for me to contact Oxoid directly. The Israelis had also identified companies from France, Switzerland, Denmark, Germany and Italy that had provided equipment and materials; for good measure, I wrote similar letters to these governments, seeking direct access to the suppliers.

Rolf Ekéus was still reminding us of the urgency to resolve the issue, so we decided we could not simply wait for answers to my letters. A few days after the Israelis had left, Dick and I were on a plane to Bahrain to meet up with the other two members of the Gang of Four, David and Hamish, before returning to Baghdad. We planned to challenge the Iraqis with the information provided by the Israelis, but at the same time were conscious that we could not give even a hint of where this intelligence had come from. We were also aware that some of it may not be correct, or if it was, it may not be related to any biological weapons program. This was going to be a tricky series of interviews, and we needed to plan it carefully.

We decided to interview thirty Iraqis on this mission, including some we had spoken to before, particularly the gentlemen from TSMID. This time we started with Dr Taha, with the TSMID gentlemen sitting next to her. Eventually we got around to the bacterial growth media imports. I still did not know how much had been imported or what types, and opened simply by asking why her defensive research program needed tonnes of bacterial growth media.

She was prepared for this, probably anticipating that sooner or later we would discover something about the imports. Nevertheless, her answer surprised me. 'It was not for my program – TSMID imported it on behalf of the Ministry of Health. They needed it for diagnostic testing, to check for diseases.'

She added for good measure, 'What I have told you is the closest to the truth regarding actual imports.' As if that was the end of the matter.

But this obviously could not be true! Diagnostic testing might consume a few grams, not tonnes. I decided to tackle this sideways. Why had TSMID imported for the Ministry of Health? We had been told that TSMID only imported for special government projects and not for authorities such as the health ministry.

Ahmed Khudayyer, the former director of TSMID, answered this one: 'They did not have the foreign exchange: it had expired.

Therefore, they resorted to another way, via TSMID. We had foreign allocations. A request was made to TSMID, and we would provide through our foreign exchange. This happens now and then. It is not an unusual occurrence.'

This answer did not gel with what we had been told previously, and I thought that I would follow up on this later with the Ministry of Health. What I really wanted to know was how much growth media was imported.

I asked, 'The quantities imported are large, whereas what Iraq has declared is small … we are looking at over 10 tonnes here. How much media did Iraq import?'

Dr Taha became defensive. 'TSMID can answer that. This is the closest to the truth that we could find. We will check … we will try to verify the figures. We will check distributed quantities.'

That afternoon, we had a representative from the Ministry of Health import division sitting across the table from us. It was Dick who opened the questioning this time, and asked why so much growth media was imported.

The representative explained, 'Iraqi orders are bigger due to supply uncertainty, so please keep this in mind. We always ask for five years supply of any item, such as spare parts. Suppliers always ask, why so much? Iraq is in an abnormal situation. During the Iran–Iraq war, we always made big orders for disposable items. Again, this is an unusual situation. We have no other recourse.'

Dick remarked, 'You must admit that these media quantities are astronomical, even for five years.'

Looking uncomfortable, the representative shrugged. 'Let us verify the quantities.' He then added cryptically, 'This was the same quantity to be used for the entire medical spectrum.'

I felt we should try to get more from the Iraqis by upping the ante. No doubt the figure they would eventually provide us with after 'checking' their records would depend on how much they thought we already knew. I had only a little extra information to push them with. The Israelis had given me two reference numbers for letters of credit, the promissory notes that banks pay out on delivery of the goods. I tried a bluff. 'Perhaps it might help if I could give you some references to the letters of credit?'

I could see this caught their interest. I had a pile of papers in a folder and, keeping them close to my chest, I leant back in my chair, pretending I was looking for copies of the actual letters of credit.

'Ah, here they are!' I said, looking at my Bahrain Holiday Inn invoices.

I carefully read out one of the Oxoid reference numbers while the Iraqis scribbled it down. I considered those on the other side of the table and contemplated whether to give them the only other reference I had, or hold it back as a check if they provided a list. I had a hand of just two aces while pretending I had a full house, but I decided to go for it.

'Here is another … I could go on.' I asked for the complete record of their letters of credit. After all, if the bacterial growth media was all for the Ministry of Health, there was no reason to destroy such documentation. My spy-school training – confidence is key – was kicking in again.

The deceit worked. The Iraqis could not be sure exactly what intelligence we had, but they decided to play it safe: it would not have gone down well with the UN Security Council if we could prove Iraq had imported media that it had refused to declare. On our last day in Baghdad, I was handed references to other bacterial growth media purchases. These revealed another 12 tonnes had been acquired from Oxoid, in addition to the 10 we already knew about. They also revealed there had been another major supplier: Fluka, a Swiss company. In all, about 37 tonnes of growth media had been purchased in 1988 and 1989, coincidentally at the same time that Dr Taha's facility, Al Hakam, was being built.

Of course, I wanted to know what had happened to all this material; as Dick had pointed out, it was an astronomical amount to use for diagnostic purposes. The Iraqis had an answer for that as well. They told us that about half of the media had been sent to pathology laboratories at seven regional hospitals. There had been riots in all these regions, and the media was stolen. The remainder was still in the Ministry of Health stores in Baghdad. In confirmation of this, he offered to provide us with Ministry of Health documentation, but this would take a few days to find and collate. I said it could be sent on to us in New York.

Dick and I returned to New York in early February 1995. Our comrades from the Gang of Four remained behind to revisit Al Hakam to see if they could pick up anything that had been missed in earlier inspections. Iraq had acknowledged that at least 37 tonnes of bacterial growth media had been imported between 1988 and 1989, of which about 17 tonnes was now missing under strange circumstances. The coincidence of the media being sent only to hospitals where riots had occurred, and the image of the theft of every single drum, had us cynically referring to the episode as 'The Great Media Riots of 1991'.

This time, Rolf accepted that we were onto something substantial. But he still felt that convincing some of the sceptical members of the UN Security Council would require more solid evidence.

Copies of the documentation I had requested arrived about a week after we returned. They comprised store receipts, store inventory cards and sales vouchers for the transfer of the media to the seven hospitals where the alleged riots had occurred. To me they seemed carefully contrived to back up Iraq's implausible story and, as 'copies', could easily have been forged. This required further investigation, starting with a request for original documentation.

I did not have to wait long. Dick made a lightning visit to Baghdad on another matter and returned with the 'originals'. I could tell almost immediately that they were fakes. The store cards, for example, which showed materials coming in and going out, were in pristine condition, not a grubby fingermark anywhere to be seen. Just as damning was that the serial numbers were all in sequence and, although the entries were months apart, the same ink appeared to have been used throughout. I remember the demonstration at spy school showing how professionals could forge a document to make it hard to distinguish from the real thing. Whoever had made the Iraqi documents would have certainly got a fail!

I decided on a more definitive test. I sent one of each of the originals to the FBI forensic division to see if they could tell how old the ink was. If I was right, it would still be oxidising.

Meanwhile, Oxoid replied to my letter, but sidestepped my request to visit their offices by simply providing more details on what they had sold to Iraq. It was a large amount, totalling some 22 tonnes, which coincided with what Iraq had acknowledged. I estimated this would have cost in the order of half a million dollars, and if used for making a bacterial warfare agent it could have produced a substantial amount – for example, tens of thousands of litres of concentrated anthrax. I phoned the Oxoid sales manager immediately and said we needed to talk directly. He invited me to visit him in the United Kingdom, an invitation I readily accepted.

The initial forensic test results came back from the FBI within a couple of weeks. Their findings were that the ink had to be no more than a couple of years old, and was probably much more recent than that. Although the FBI promised more definitive tests, the initial findings were good enough for me. The ink did not match the dates written on the documents by many years, and this was proof they were fakes.

Rolf was to address the Security Council on the status of Iraq's disarmament later that morning, so I went to see him. I felt the evidence was now 'solid'. Iraq had imported at least 37 tonnes of bacterial growth media, 17 tonnes of which was missing. Not only was the explanation for the missing material unbelievable, we now had evidence that the documentation provided to back up the story had been forged.

I handed Rolf the documents, suggesting that he strengthen his presentation on Iraq's biological weapons program by holding them up, declaring them to be fakes. I could see him weighing up the pros and cons of this piece of theatrics, but in the end he decided against it. He did, though, manage to convince the Security Council, including the Russians, that 17 tonnes of unaccounted-for bacterial growth media imported by Iraq was a serious matter, and Iraq had some questions to answer.

Rolf's presentation became headline news in the US press the following day. More importantly, it bought us a bit more time to complete the investigation.

* * *

I had been planning to visit Oxoid the following week, but now I put that on hold. The heat was on Iraq after Rolf's presentation, and I felt I should return immediately to follow up on the missing media. I had been planning a mission with a small team of inspectors to visit places such as the Iraqi customs document repository, the Ministry of Health and the Ministry of Trade to search for documents that might shed more light on the import of the bacterial growth media and its fate. This inspection was the ideal hook to quiz the Iraqis about the forged documents.

I left New York for Baghdad on 8 March 1995. My first stop was the Ministry of Health headquarters in downtown Baghdad. I wanted to test what I had been told by the director of TSMID just a few weeks earlier. Had the Ministry of Health run out of foreign exchange currency and asked TSMID for the use of their funds?

I spoke with the head of the ministry's financial department while the rest of my team waded through mountains of documents on imports. I was not surprised when he told me that he had never heard of TSMID and, in any case, borrowing credit from another department would not have been permitted under Iraqi financial rules. So much for the director of TSMID's comment that it was not an unusual occurrence.

The person I really wanted to speak to was the head storeman for the Ministry of Health. If Iraq's story was true, it would be his handwriting on the documents. I requested a meeting.

That evening, the meeting took place. A few senior members of my team sat on one side of the table, and on the other sat the storeman, Abdul Razzack. In his early fifties, bespectacled and slightly stooped, he at least looked like a storeman. On either side of him were the usual Iraq minders, with Dr Taha sitting next to him. This was going to be interesting.

I began with some basic questions, including whether he had written the receipts for the incoming growth media. He confirmed that he had. But before I could move on to when he had done this, he volunteered that they were 'reconstructed' from the originals a couple of years ago.

'So, let me get this straight,' I said. 'The documents handed to us were not true originals?'

'Yes, they were,' countered the storeman. 'They were reconstructed originals.'

This was getting weird. I felt the Iraqis were now digging the hole even deeper. I was compelled to ask what seemed, even to me, a strange question. 'What happened to the original originals?'

The storeman explained that there had been a fire and the 'original originals' had been lost in the flames. This raised the obvious question of how he had managed to draw up the 'reconstructed originals'. How could he possibly remember the precise dates and quantities of material coming into his store to create the new receipt cards? He told me that, fortunately, he had put the details in his notebook before the fire and he used this as the basis. It came as no surprise when he related that he had lost his notebook and therefore could not show it to me.

The following day, the team and I visited the scene of the alleged fire, a document store in the north of Baghdad. Clearly the Iraqis had not prepared the site, because there was no evidence of a fire, no report of attendance by the fire services on the alleged date and no damage to any of the other documents in the store. The best explanation that Abdul Razzack could offer was that it was a very small fire caused by a faulty electrical cable falling onto the steel cabinet where the receipts were stored. It destroyed only them.

The whole story was becoming more and more absurd, but it was not over yet.

The next day, we visited the Department of Health store, where the media was said to have been kept. Sure enough, there were drums of media from Oxoid, about 11 tonnes of it.

I took this opportunity with Abdul Razzack. 'Yesterday we saw where the store receipts met their fiery end. I would now like to ask you about the sales vouchers to the seven hospitals. They could not have been destroyed along with the receipts because, as I understand it, they were kept in a different location. Are the vouchers that were passed to us originals?'

'Yes, they are original,' he replied, but then added, 'They are original copies.'

Of course, I asked what had happened to the originals on this occasion.

'We had to move all the documents on a truck to another store, and a box fell off. The sales vouchers were in the box.'

I could not resist: 'Are you now telling me that the vouchers *fell off the back of a truck*?'

'Yes, the vouchers fell off the back of a truck.'

I had deliberately put words into his mouth, but I was thinking ahead to how I would present all this in New York. The story was so nonsensical that I wanted to make the greatest impact possible in my reporting of this absurdity.

Before we left Baghdad, we had a final meeting with the Iraqis, including Dr Taha and Abdul Razzack. I had further questions about the documentation and went systematically and laboriously through the details. The more I probed, the more inconsistencies appeared. After about half an hour of this farce, we reached a point at which the frightened storeman did not know how to respond. I felt sorry for him, seated between the Iraqi minders and Dr Taha, but I needed to demonstrate to the Iraqi side that their story was unsustainable. To leave no doubt in their minds of the consequences of what we had heard over the last few days, I said, 'We do not find the story of the documentation at all credible. Although we have not come to a final conclusion, all the evidence points to the documents being false. I ask you to consider providing us with a more coherent and verifiable story explaining the fate of the bacterial growth media. Otherwise, we have no choice but to write an adverse report reflecting our findings.'

For once, there was no retort from the other side. They all knew that an 'adverse report' would mean no lifting of the sanctions and, after the recent presentation by Rolf on the missing 17 tonnes of media, almost certainly the loss of support by the few friends they had on the UN Security Council.

The next day, I was in Bahrain again, expecting to return to New York, but instead I was met by Rolf, Dick and a few others from UNSCOM. It seemed that Iraq was aware that the bacterial growth media was a serious problem for them and had called a high-level meeting with the United Nations in an attempt to resolve it.

The Iraqis were to be led by General Amer Rashid, whom I had met on a number of occasions. He was an engineer by profession and at one time was head of Iraq's missile program, which developed the rockets that struck Tel Aviv during the Gulf War. He was now the go-between for Saddam Hussein and the United Nations. He was a tall man of solid build, great intellect and, on occasion, some wit. But his most striking feature was his piercing eyes, which seemed to try to pin his adversaries. He was boastful, with a bullying personality, and more than once I had seen him lose his temper. He was not a man to cross, especially if you were an Iraqi.

On the evening of our arrival in Baghdad, Rolf had a tête-à-tête with General Rashid, who told him that Iraq was sticking to its story that it never had a biological weapons program. Rashid said that Saddam had told him that Iraq 'will cooperate with the commission – no matter what happens, we will cooperate. In biology they may say "we did it", but they say that only to silence us.'

The latter part of the message seemed cryptic, but that was so often the way with Saddam.

Now our investigations were at the point where we could contradict Saddam, and say 'they did it'. While I had been pursuing the growth media, Hamish and David had built up a picture of what Al Hakam might really be for – and that was not to produce yeast. While none of it was definitive, it certainly appeared to us from equipment purchases, along with the deception and secrecy surrounding Al Hakam, that it had been built as a biological weapons plant. The media purchases coinciding with the acquisition of equipment, and their ridiculous denials of a link, seemed to confirm this. It was going to be an interesting meeting with Rashid.

We met with the Iraqis the following morning. On one side of a long conference table sat General Amer Rashid, Dr Taha and an assortment of other officials. Significantly, this meeting was attended by Iraq's deputy foreign minister, Dr Riyadh Al-Qaysi. He was a diminutive man who spoke impeccable English in gentle tones but for all that, had little to say. I later understood that he was there to weigh the arguments of both sides to see if Iraq could bluff its way through. He was like an adjudicator, or a judge for Saddam.

Dick and others presented UNSCOM's views on the inconsistences of Iraq's so-called defensive program and on Al Hakam. We avoided discussing the growth media, except for a brief mention. We wanted to show the Iraqis that our case was broader than just the missing growth media.

Dr Taha looked slightly ill when we finished, especially since she knew this was only part of our case. Rashid, clearly agitated, shouted, 'You should not listen to the lies that countries tell you. The intelligence you have been given has misled you – you should use Iraqi information to support your conclusions! I tell you, there is no evidence that is contrary to our declaration.'

I wondered momentarily whether Iraqis had uncovered our contacts with Israeli intelligence, and perhaps even my intelligence background. However, I decided that if Amer Rashid had this information, he would have accused me more directly, so I dismissed his reference to intelligence as general bluster.

He addressed the growth media. 'You know, this media was ordered for one year for all the hospitals in Iraq. This was 1 tonne. Then his boss said, "Let's make that five years." So now it was 5 tonnes.

And then that man's boss said, "Let's play safe and double it." So, 10 tonnes. Then his boss, and his boss, doubled it again, so through these idiots we finished up with 40 tonnes. It was a one-off mistake.'

To all of us at UNSCOM, this came as a new explanation of the acquisition of the growth media. It was also almost as bizarre as the other explanations the Iraqis had provided, but we listened politely.

Amer Rashid promised that everything would become clear after Dr Taha gave her presentation, scheduled for that evening. 'She will demolish your arguments.'

I couldn't wait.

* * *

Dr Taha began at 7.40 pm that evening. I noticed Dr Al-Qaysi listened intently to every word.

She began with a brief description of how the growth media was purchased for the Ministry of Health. Any missing media could not possibly have been used by Al Hakam, she said, because the facility did not have that capacity. She moved to a whiteboard set up behind the row of Iraqi officials to show her calculations to justify her claim. She began scribbling numbers and equations on the board, and within less than a minute, had lost her audience, except for Dick and me. We could just about follow her reasoning, although we could each recognise technical flaws in her arguments.

She continued on in this manner for the next half hour. I glanced at Dr Al-Qaysi and could see the confusion on his face. Eventually, she finished triumphantly: 'And therefore, Al Hakam could not have consumed 17 tonnes of growth media.'

Dr Taha had avoided any mention of the ridiculous story of the theft of the missing 17 tonnes and of the 'reconstructed' documentation they had given us to back this up. By now, I think both Rashid and Taha knew this was a losing horse.

Dr Taha addressed a few other issues we had raised about Al Hakam. The meeting finished at about 11.30 and, apart from a few comments from us, had consisted almost entirely of her voice. Our turn would come the next evening, when I would present our views.

The following day, Dick and I discussed how I would counter Dr Taha. We were aware that I would be talking to a non-technical audience, and it was vital that they could follow the arguments. I decided that it was important not to correct the scientific errors in Taha's case; I could foresee General Rashid dismissing our views as 'differences of opinion on the technicalities'. In the end, I decided not to address what Dr Taha had said at all.

That evening, both sides sat across the conference table in a tense silence. Everyone knew this was a critical moment for Iraq. If my presentation was convincing, Iraq's denials of a biological weapons program would be unsustainable. At the very least, it would mean that the vast complex built at Al Hakam would have to be destroyed. I was only too aware of the importance of the moment. Dr Al-Qaysi was sitting quietly to one side, watching me intensely.

I had given many technical presentations to non-technical audiences and was confident in my skills. Anything even slightly technical, I explained carefully and simply, without going into too much detail. I could see that the audience was following me.

I had decided that, to make the presentation more compelling, I would give a worked example of how much anthrax Al Hakam could have theoretically produced, given the fermenters and other equipment there. I had not got very far into this when, from my position at the whiteboard, I heard Dr Taha behind me, raising objections. I knew this disruption was a tactic and decided to ignore her. I did not want to break my rhythm by getting into an argument.

The final part of my presentation dealt with how much bacteria growth media Al Hakam would have consumed if it had made anthrax, and neatly came up with a figure of 17 tonnes. I concluded, 'This, of course, would explain why 17 tonnes of media is missing.'

When I was finished, there was silence in the room, except for some indecipherable noise from Dr Taha. I turned around and, to my shock, saw that she was sobbing.

The silence did not last long. General Amer Rashid bellowed a stream of invective at me. I do not recall it all, but there was a mixture of threats and allegations of lies.

I was shocked by his overreaction. I thought it wise to resume my seat on the other side of the table, across from General Rashid. He did not let up, jabbing his finger at me, berating me with the words 'outrageous' and 'lies', and probably 'outrageous lies'. I tried to keep stony-faced as his tirade continued. But I was also pleased with both Dr Taha's and General Rashid's response. If this was their best counter, Iraq had lost the battle. I looked over to Dr Al-Qaysi and saw the resignation on his face.

Eventually, Rolf intervened and called for calm. He too looked stunned. Although we had told him of Dr Taha's breakdown in response to David Kelly's questioning, this was the first time he had witnessed her tears himself. And while we had all seen angry outbursts from Rashid before, the intensity here was up a notch or two.

After a short break, there was some discussion about my presentation, another outburst from General Amer Rashid and a few more tears from Dr Taha. But we had won, and no histrionics from those two were going to change that.

* * *

Back in New York, the Gang of Four met up. We all agreed we could not simply cool our heels waiting to see what Iraq might do next. I wondered what was going on behind the scenes. Dick and I had assumed the outbursts from General Rashid and Dr Taha were because we had caught them out. But they had been rather clumsy, and this would not have gone down well with Saddam. Perhaps this explained Dr Taha's tears; she would know the consequences of failure in such a brutal regime.

We decided that our little team would divide: Hamish and David would return to Iraq as soon as possible for an extensive sampling mission at Al Hakam, in the hope they could pick up traces of anthrax from the fermenters or drains. Dick would talk to some anthrax experts in the United States, while I would visit Oxoid in the United Kingdom.

I left for London on 5 April 1995. My first stop was the Defence Intelligence Service, where I had been the Australian intelligence liaison officer. Although I was on secondment to UNSCOM, officially I was still the Director of Strategic Technology at DIO in Canberra and so still had all the relevant clearances to talk at the top-secret level. I went to see my counterpart in the DIS, Dr Brian Jones, the director of intelligence for nuclear, biological and chemical weapons systems, whom I knew well. I wanted to talk to Brian and his staff to see if they had any intelligence I might have missed, but it soon became clear that we in New York were far ahead of the United Kingdom. No matter how good a nation's spies might be, it is hard to beat the person on the ground.

The next morning, I met with Oxoid's sales manager. I asked about Iraq's purchases and was shown a file establishing that TSMID had bought 22 tonnes of bacterial growth media in 1988. He explained that normally these files would have been shredded after five years, but he thought the orders were so unusual he kept them.

He also showed me other regular purchases made by Iraq, right up to the start of the Gulf War in 1991. Iraq's Ministry of Health had placed orders for small quantities of diagnostic media, the type used by hospitals for identifying bacteria responsible for diseases and infections. This information completely demolished Iraq's story that TSMID had purchased the tonnes of media on behalf of its health ministry.

After my meeting with the sales manager, I was given a comprehensive tour of the plant. Oxoid had been very helpful in my investigation, and the intelligence I collected there could be valuable if Iraq persisted with its cover story.

Before leaving, I dropped by the sales manager's office to thank him and ask a delicate question that had been bugging me. What did he think Iraq had been buying 22 tonnes of media for? He answered that he assumed Iraq had started an antibiotic production plant or similar, but had found it a bit odd; that's why he had kept the sales records. I left it at that.

My trip to Oxoid was followed by a mini Grand Tour. In response to letters I had sent out in January, I had received invitations to visit suppliers in about half a dozen countries. I met up with Dick in Copenhagen, and for the next couple of weeks we zigzagged across Europe to see suppliers of equipment and materials. In Switzerland, we visited Fluka, the other company we knew had supplied bacterial growth media to Iraq, and collected copies of orders from TSMID and a series of sales documents. This was the hard evidence we had been seeking, and most of it backed up the Israeli intelligence.

As at Oxoid, I always asked the question about what the sales reps had thought Iraq was going to do with these supplies. At one company the answer was given by their lawyer, who simply told me, 'There were no restrictions at the time. We did not break any laws.'

This was probably true, because the Australia Group controls had not been implemented then. Nevertheless, the technical experts in the room just stared down at their hands, trying not to make eye contact. I guessed they had had their suspicions about what the materials were for, but in the end, business is business.

It was good to return to New York. It was early May 1995 and the doorman to my apartment barely recognised me, so rarely had I been there over the past few months, but at least he allowed me up to see my beautiful Jan. However, I had little time to recuperate, as the Iraqis suggested another meeting in Baghdad, and Rolf thought that Dick and I should accompany him. We all speculated that the Iraqis might now confess to having had a biological weapons program at Al Hakam. But experience had taught us we could never be sure which way they would flip.

The meeting was scheduled for mid-May, which gave Dick and me just enough time to visit Israeli intelligence in Tel Aviv to see if they had anything more to strengthen our case. But we had exhausted their supply of intelligence, and I realised that, just as with British intelligence, we knew vastly more about Iraq's biological weapons program than they did.

Rolf met with Deputy Prime Minister Tariq Aziz in Baghdad, but any hope of a confession dissipated within the first minute. Aziz told Rolf that Iraq had cooperated fully with UNSCOM on all matters and wanted a clean bill of health so that sanctions could be lifted. They had nothing further to add on the matter of a biological weapons program.

This was, to say the least, disappointing.

Dick and I thought we would challenge the Iraqis with the new information from our trip to Europe. Since the intel we had gained was not from intelligence agencies, we could be more open with the Iraqis about our sources. We were not optimistic that it would elicit anything after Tariq Aziz's edict, but it would at least show Iraq that we held a strong hand.

But General Rashid would not countenance this, and stated bluntly that Dick and I were not welcome to seek meetings with any Iraqi officials. Neither Dr Taha nor any other Iraqi official would be permitted to talk to us.

We checked out of our hotel the following morning. Leaving was not so easy. First, we had to walk a gauntlet of protesters – allegedly doctors and nurses – waving placards saying *UN kills babies* and, worse still, holding up very sick babies. They were chanting, 'Down with the US, down with the UN' and 'Lies!' Some were waving their fists at us. I had seen similar demonstrations in Iraq before, but this was up close and personal. No doubt it was a rent-a-crowd. Although I didn't believe we would be physically attacked, there was always the risk that someone would get carried away.

Unusually, the Iraqi government had provided a car to take us to the airport. The big old Chevrolet was waiting not next to the entrance but on the far side of the carpark, and we had to gently push our way through the mob to the vehicle. It didn't stop when we got in, with demonstrators banging on the roof and windscreen. If we hadn't already got General Rashid's message that we were not welcome, we had now.

I am not sure what Iraq's objective was in treating Dick and me this way during our short stay in Baghdad. The problem they had over the biological weapons program was not going to disappear by stonewalling us, and the attempts at intimidation were not going to end our investigations. It could, of course, just have been to show Saddam that they were doing something. But whatever the rationale, it soon backfired on them.

When Rolf returned to New York, he presented a brief to the UN Security Council on this latest trip. He told the council that Iraq had refused to meet with Dick and me. He revealed the new information we had gained in Europe, and concluded, 'The evidence available to the commission establishes that Iraq obtained or sought to obtain all the items and materials required to produce biological warfare agents in Iraq. With Iraq's failure to account for all those items and material for legitimate purposes, the only conclusion that can be drawn is that there is a high risk that Iraq purchased them and used them at least in part for proscribed purposes – the production of agents for biological weapons.'

Stronger words could have been used, but in the world of diplomacy this was strong enough. The ensuing debate in the Council did not go well for Iraq, and the unanimous decision was that Iraq needed to cooperate and provide explanations for this latest evidence.

This time, it was Rolf who called General Rashid to suggest a meeting. Rashid immediately agreed and invited Rolf, Dick and me to visit at the end of June 1995. He added that he would like to make 'a statement'. Was this the end?

* * *

On the morning of 1 July 1995, we met with the Iraqis in the executive conference room in Iraq's Ministry of Defence. As usual, the UN delegation sat on one side of a long table, Rolf in the centre, with Dick and I flanking him. Opposite us sat the Iraqi officials, General Amer in the centre and Dr Taha perched alongside him. I noticed that at the far end of the Iraqi line was Dr Al-Qaysi, his hands clasped on the table and his head slightly bowed. I sensed that this might be a meeting at which we would at last hear the confession we had been working to elicit over the last six months.

Just before arriving, we had learned that General Rashid had been promoted to the Minister of Oil. He must have done something right in Saddam's eyes: in oil-rich Iraq, this was one of the most powerful political positions in the country. We had also learned that he had married Dr Taha. The former head of Iraq's deadly missile program had married the person we believed was the former head of Iraq's deadly biological weapons program. It might be love, but it could also be something more sinister. Briefly, I entertained the thought that they could be holding hands under the table.

After a short introduction, General Rashid leaned over to his wife and gently asked her to read the prepared statement in front of her. In a somewhat quavering voice, she began slowly. 'To clarify the beginning of the biological program, we state here that the program began at the end of 1985 at Al Muthanna State Establishment. At that time Dr Rihab Taha was working on bio-pesticides in the aforementioned establishment.'

I knew Al Muthanna well: it was the chemical weapons plant that was the subject of UNSCOM's first inspection and which, as an intelligence officer in DIO, I had studied for many years prior to that. I was a little surprised to learn that the biological weapons program had started there. We certainly had no inkling of this from an intelligence point of view.

Dr Taha continued to provide details of the early days of Iraq's 'biological program'. I was uncertain if she was referring to a 'defensive' program or actually admitting to a weapons program. The formality of the language and the reference to herself in the third person struck me. It seemed as if the statement had been written by lawyers.

After about ten minutes, the big moment came. 'In the first quarter of 1988, and after the success of research in relation to *Clostridium botulinum* (botulinum toxin) and *Bacillus anthracis* (anthrax), a decision was adopted to prepare the requirements for producing biological agents.'

Before she could continue, Rashid turned to her and said, in a surprisingly tender tone, 'No, not biological agents. Biological *warfare* agents.'

Taha met his eyes briefly and read the sentence again with the insertion.

These were the words that our side had been waiting for. Iraq had at last admitted to running a biological weapons program.

Dr Taha offered more details, explaining how Al Hakam had been set up as a production plant for anthrax and botulinum toxin.

A couple of times, she again read the words 'biological agent', and Rashid again gently gave the correction. She gave figures for the quantity of agents produced: 9000 litres of botulinum toxin and 600 litres of concentrated anthrax. This had consumed about 15 tonnes of the bacterial growth media acquired from Oxoid and Fluka.

She finished by telling us that all the anthrax and botulinum toxin had been destroyed in October 1990. Falling into silence, she looked up from the paper and glanced at her husband, perhaps looking for his approval. He responded with an almost imperceptible nod. She then turned to us, waiting for a response.

This had been a confession, but certainly not a true confession. Yes, she had admitted to a biological weapons program, acknowledged the role of Al Hakam and accounted for most of the missing media. But why, after all the effort and expense, were the biological weapons agents destroyed before the Gulf War, and the program abandoned? This would be the time when such a weapons system might be needed. What struck me just as forcefully was the lack of any reference to any weapons. Surely they had bombs or rockets filled with the stuff?

After a moment or two, Rolf spoke for our side. 'What about the munitions?' he asked.

Dr Taha responded immediately, 'No. Never. There was not time enough to carry on with munitions.'

Rashid helped her out. 'With the events of August 1990' – referring to the invasion of Kuwait – 'we could not have possibly embarked on this course. We wanted to prove that we could produce the agent, but weapons did not materialise.'

Both sides agreed to meet that evening to work through Taha's statement with some of Iraq's technical experts. But we could not elicit any further information from the Iraqi side. They seemed to be back to their old tricks, not admitting to anything they did not have to concede. I was beginning to question how much of what we had heard, beyond the existence of a biological weapons program, was actually true.

The munitions issue was the most disturbing aspect. Were bombs filled with anthrax still out there? This was a question we returned to time and time again. Eventually, a leading Iraqi scientist, exasperated with our probing, waved his hands in the air and said, 'You must understand that this is political. It is all political.'

We took this thought back to New York with us the following day. There were some things Iraq was not going to reveal, probably under instruction from Saddam himself. Nevertheless, we had had a victory of sorts, and the consequence of that, under the UN Security Council resolution following the Gulf War, was that everything at Al Hakam would need to be destroyed. This included all the equipment, any remaining bacterial growth media and even the buildings, so that Iraq could not simply resume a biological weapons program at a later date.

The partial victory also meant that there was a lot more investigation to do. As it turned out, the Gang of Four would work on this for the next three to four years, slowly piecing together the greater extent of the program.

I thought back once more to the briefing I had given Bob Hawke at the start of the Gulf War. I had implied that there was little to worry about as far as biological weapons were concerned. I had also told him that Iraq was probably decades away from a nuclear bomb. The truth was just the opposite. At least my brief on chemical weapons had been correct. I tried to console myself that one out of three ain't bad.

Uncovering Iraq's biological weapons program had taken us six months. We had had a lucky break with the leads provided by Israeli intelligence, but I believe we would have got there eventually even without those leads. As with many intelligence riddles, it was a matter of knowing where to look. In this case, the answers were not in Iraq but in the countries where the suppliers were. Ironically, the seedstock for the most deadly strain of anthrax produced by Iraq was supplied by a US company. You never know what an intelligence investigation may discover.

CHAPTER 8

THE FREE AGENT

> 'The biggest risk is not taking any risk ... In a world that is changing really quickly, the only strategy that is guaranteed to fail is not taking risks.'
>
> Mark Zuckerberg

My secondment to the United Nations had spun out from six months to two years, and I had become anxious about my job in Canberra. Because of my prolonged absence, someone else was appointed as Director of Strategic Technology in early 1996. I wondered whether I still had a job in intelligence. Jan and I decided it was time to go home.

I had a new boss, Major General Jim Connolly, whom I had written to from New York shortly after his appointment to introduce myself. Upon my return to DIO, I thought it would be a good idea to stop by his office to meet him.

Things began awkwardly. 'Good morning, General Connolly,' I said, extending my hand. 'I'm Rod Barton. You may recall that I wrote to you recently about what I've been doing over the past couple of years.'

He took my hand but looked blank. After a moment or two,

obviously trying to work out who I was, he simply asked, 'I'm sorry?'

But we soon got chatting, more about Somalia than Iraq. I was not surprised to learn that neither he nor anyone else seemed to have given much thought to my role on my return. I was beginning to fear that before long I would be transferred out of intelligence and into some backwater in the Defence department.

During my time away, there had been a shift in DIO, to focus more on Australia's immediate region rather than the Middle East and global issues such as weapons of mass destruction. As a stop-gap measure, I suggested to General Connolly that I could write some 'lessons learned' papers on the Iraq saga that might have wider application for the intelligence community. He seized on this, perhaps to disguise that he had no other plans for me.

I spent the next few days wandering the corridors of DIO, looking for an office and a desk. At least here, unlike in Somalia, I wouldn't have to bribe an official to get these basics.

I barely had time to settle into my new office when the United Nations asked me to return for a few weeks to help with resolving the remaining issues on Iraq's biological warfare program. Soon I was back with the Gang of Four, and my comings and goings – a few weeks in Iraq at a time – continued for the next six months. In between, I worked on the 'lessons learned' papers. It was a strange existence, made stranger at times by the events going on in Iraq. It seemed that we still had much to learn.

Saddam's son-in-law and heir apparent, Hussein Kamel Hassan al-Majid, had defected to the West in August 1995, and this had caused some political turmoil. We were told that he was the one who had made the decisions on the acquisition of the bacterial growth media, and that was followed by the fiasco of not fully declaring Iraq's biological program. His failure on these matters had precipitated his defection to Jordan. For us, his defection was good news, as he readily agreed to talk to us about Iraq's secret weapons programs.

Strangely, he decided to return to Iraq early in 1996, after assurances from the devious Saddam he would not be harmed. Upon return he was, perhaps predictably, arrested, jailed and tortured, and died a gruesome death. This was followed by political turmoil within Iraq's inner circles that also had consequences for the inspection process. Iraq's approach to inspections became even more erratic, at times cooperative and at others, highly combative.

During one of Iraq's more cooperative moments, Iraqi officials led us to a stash of papers, photographs and videos hidden at a farm. We were told that Hussein Kamal had hidden them there so that if Iraq's weapons programs were to be resumed in future, the know-how would not be lost. Whether that was true, we were keen to get these documents out of the country as quickly as possible, in case the mood changed.

In one of his rare direct instructions, Rolf tasked me to collect the documents and get them back to New York pronto. I was not to let them out of my sight. I was not to have them loaded into the hold of an aircraft, just in case ...

The first stage of the journey was to get them from Baghdad to Bahrain. I re-packed the documents in a small, nondescript bag so as not to raise suspicions when carrying them out of my hotel. A special flight had been arranged by our Luftwaffe friends in one of their military transports to take me, with Hamish riding shotgun, to Bahrain. So far, so good.

But the journey to Bahrain did not go smoothly. Halfway into the flight, one of the two engines lost power, and we had an emergency landing in Kuwait. Clutching my little bag of documents, I was led with the others to the Kuwaiti Air Force officers' lounge, where we spent a few hours talking about Iraq, the war and inspections. Eventually, the Germans organised a back-up plane and we continued on.

At Bahrain International Airport, I had to do some quick talking to a supervisor at British Airways. My small bag was still larger than they would allow as carry-on. In the end, I confided the nature of the contents. The supervisor relented straight away and made arrangements for me to travel first class. At least there were some advantages to being a courier.

Hamish and I examined the cache in great detail in New York. It was the sort of intelligence analysis work we both had years of experience in, and we relished the task. The documents did not give us a comprehensive picture of what the Iraqis had been up to, but did provide some valuable leads. Some of the videos showed munition trials of bombs and rockets filled with biological agents, and Hamish, as a military engineer, used these to plan future inspections. In fact, there were many bits and pieces that the Gang of Four would follow up on in the coming months. Perhaps the documents were more of a silver mine than a gold mine, but they were nevertheless valuable.

The hidden stash of documents revealed that more bacterial growth media had been imported than Iraq had publicly acknowledged. I was keen to talk to Dr Taha about this. Dick and I arranged a visit to Baghdad to follow up on the new leads.

General Rashid held a reception for us just after our arrival. Unexpected, to say the least. We had informed him of the general nature of our mission, so he knew that I would soon be talking to his wife about the bacterial growth media. When he took me aside at the reception, I wondered if he wanted to ask me about this. Instead, and with a smile on his face, he told me, 'Dr Barton, many people here welcome you.'

I beamed back at this apparent good news.

Then, fixing me with his steely gaze, he lowered his voice and added, chillingly, 'But many here would prefer to see you dead.'

I took this as a threat on my life. In Iraq, when references to your death are made by someone like Rashid, no matter how obliquely, they are not to be dismissed.

My questioning of Dr Taha later that day brought forth more tears, not because of any aggressiveness on my behalf, but because, I assumed, I had again hit on a truth that Taha could not confess upon pain of death. I wondered how our interview went down with her husband that evening.

* * *

Back in Canberra, there was little interest in the goings-on in Iraq or my work with UNSCOM. I returned from one mission in May 1996 and passed General Connolly on the stairs as I was going down and he was going up. He asked me how it had gone. It had actually been unusually difficult, with many tensions following a purge of six generals by Saddam. I looked Connolly in the eye and said slowly, 'You know, in Iraq, they shoot generals.'

He saw the humour and quickly responded with, 'Ah, but they were all lieutenant generals. I'm only a major general!'

We both had a chuckle and I thought, *well, at least he has some idea what's happening there.*

I knew that sooner or later DIO would tire of my comings and goings. After all, the organisation was still paying my wages. So when the Australian public service began downsizing, I took a redundancy. I had finished the three 'lessons learned' papers that I had promised and presented these to yet another new boss, Major General Bill Crews. He seemed grateful but, like his predecessor, also a bit puzzled about who I was. It was obviously time to leave the intelligence service and become a free agent.

The United Nations still seemed to want my services. My intelligence experience had proved valuable in tracking down the biological growth media, but the story was not finished. While the others in the Gang of Four focused on matters in their fields of speciality, I decided I would try to discover what had happened to a few tonnes of growth media that still seemed unaccounted for. I had become aware through the intelligence I collected on imports that there was a possibility Iraq had not fully declared all the types of biological weapons it had made. This needed to be resolved.

I immediately hit a problem I had not anticipated. The United Nations wrote to the Australian government, requesting my services, but were rebuffed because I was no longer in government employ. So for a while I was caught in a sort of limbo: with no endorsement by the government, the United Nations would not take me back. Major General Crews saw the dilemma, and through an informal arrangement he supported my continued participation with UNSCOM. Although I would not be paid, I was prepared to accept this, as the work was challenging and interesting. So, for the next two years, I worked for no pay, with only my allowances covered by the United Nations. Being a free agent has its downside!

Bit by bit we, the Gang of Four, uncovered the outstanding details of Iraq's biological weapons program. There were a couple of issues that we could not resolve by traditional intelligence techniques. One was the couple of tonnes of bacterial growth media still missing. Had Iraq used this to make more anthrax than they had told us about and squirrelled it away somewhere? The other, more serious issue that stumped us all was whether Iraq had actually destroyed any of its declared bacterial agents. We had investigated the site where they said they had destroyed an agent extensively, but there were anomalies, and the evidence seemed to suggest that what we had been told was not true.

Before we could finish our investigations, events overtook us. Towards the end of 1998, Iraq had had enough of the Gang of Four, and indeed enough of the United Nations in general. Its cooperation became spasmodic. Of course, all this was reported to the UN Security Council, and that in turn resulted in almost immediate military action. On 16 December 1998, the United States and the United Kingdom launched Operation Desert Fox, a bombing campaign against Iraq that destroyed a few military establishments, factories and research facilities.

I felt strongly that this was not the way to go. Iraqi lives were lost and the raids did little to address any capability that Iraq may have had in making prohibited weapons. As a free agent, I now felt able to express my views publicly, and I wrote an article for *The New York Times*. I had kept up my contacts with the CIA and was almost certain that its analysts knew less than we did. I therefore felt confident in writing: '[t]he damage done to Iraq's weapons capabilities is probably marginal. It is almost certain that no bomb hit hidden stockpiles of chemical or biological bombs. UNSCOM had been searching for years for such arsenals, and if the inspectors had not found them, then it is unlikely that the US, even with its impressive intelligence resources, would know where they were.'

After Operation Desert Fox, Iraq's deputy prime minister announced that UN inspectors would never again set foot in Iraq. Tariq Aziz saw many of us as spies (which some of us were!), and was glad to see the back of us even if it meant that sanctions would not be lifted. I imagine he believed that enough under-the-table deals could be done to continue to sell oil in exchange for goods, thereby circumventing sanction controls.

Even though there were to be no further missions into Iraq, the Gang of Four did not quite disperse. Throughout 1999 we were invited to New York from time to time to record everything we had learnt about Iraq's biological weapons program and how we had uncovered it. The United Nations thought this might be useful if in future circumstances changed.

In October that year, there was discussion in the UN Security Council of abolishing UNSCOM and creating a new and less intrusive monitoring regime for Iraq, to begin early in 2000. In one sense, any new monitoring organisation would be theoretical, since Iraq had not relented its stance and the United Nations was still barred from the country.

The UN finally ended UNSCOM's mandate in December 1999, and this marked the formal end of the Gang of Four. We had one last dinner together in New York and, over a glass of wine, I asked my colleagues if they would they join the mooted watered-down replacement of UNSCOM if they were invited. The answers were predictable. Dick outright refused to become involved with what he called a sham organisation only there for political reasons. David Kelly, who was employed by the British Foreign Office, was reluctant but cautious, adding that as a dutiful civil servant, if the British government asked him, he would. Hamish, like me, said he would 'wait and see'.

At the end of the night, we shook hands and said our goodbyes. We all thought that this might be the end of our involvement with Iraq and the hunt for the missing elements of its biological weapons program. And for some of us, it was.

CHAPTER 9

A SPECIAL ADVISOR

'I think that my darkest moment was the Iraq war and the fact that we could not stop it.'

Kofi Annan

As the new millennium dawned, I was back in Canberra, an unemployed free agent. Jan landed a posting to Washington, D.C., as part of the Australian intelligence team liaising with the CIA and the FBI. In some ways, the liaison team's work was similar to what I had been doing in London some ten years earlier. I went with her to Washington for a few months, before commitments called me home.

My main reason to return to Australia was to appear before two parliamentary inquiries. One was on Australian relations with the Middle East, and I gave my views on Iraq. In August 2000, I told the Joint Standing Committee on Foreign Affairs, Defence and Trade that, while there were still issues to resolve, Iraq was effectively disarmed: 'Largely through the work of UNSCOM, much of Iraq's capabilities in [missile, nuclear, chemical, biological] fields have been eliminated. While it is not possible to be too definitive as to exactly what percentage of Iraq's capabilities have been eliminated, it is probably in the vicinity of 95 per cent or more.'

I stated that, as DIO's former Director of Strategic Technology and a former UN weapons inspector, I was reasonably confident that whatever was left of Iraq's weapons program was now, due to the passage of time, largely ineffective. In other words, Iraq was not a significant threat. Our relationship with the country should be based on that premise.

I received a good reception from the committee. During a coffee break, I was chatting with the chairperson and happened to mention that my partner was in Washington and I would soon be returning there. She asked if I might visit New York to talk to the head of the new organisation that had replaced UNSCOM. It was called the United Nations Monitoring, Verification and Inspection Commission on Iraq, UNMOVIC, and was headed by Dr Hans Blix, a former Swedish foreign minister and a former head of nuclear watchdog the International Atomic Energy Agency.

I was curious about the new outfit headed by Blix. Was it as watered down as we, the Gang of Four, suspected? What was its future now that Iraq had banned the United Nations from the country? What was Blix, who had an excellent international reputation, doing in it? I readily agreed to the chairperson's request.

First, though, I had other commitments in the United States, including a couple of public lectures, one at Harvard in Boston and the other at the Carnegie Foundation in Washington. I could now express my views on Iraq without too much restriction, and some of these views found their way into US news outlets.

It was not until early 2001 that Jan and I landed in New York, in the depths of an icy winter. I had not been sure that Blix would even agree to see me, an itinerant Australian not connected to an organisation, but I discovered that he had read press reports of my recent talks and was pleased that someone was raising the status of Iraq's weapons program in the media. His secretary had made an appointment for the very morning of my arrival.

The burning question I had was what Blix's organisation was doing. Iraq was still not allowing inspectors into the country, and with the lack of international interest, there was no pressure on the Iraqi government to change its mind. UNMOVIC's relevance had become questionable. I too wondered whether a group of inspectors sitting in an office in New York had any future.

Blix, though, had a new approach. With his lawyer's mind, he had decided that if the disarmament problems with Iraq were ever to be resolved, each issue had to be clearly analysed and defined. Following that, UNMOVIC would need to work out precisely what was required from Iraq to satisfy the United Nations. So far, his inspectors had identified more than 100 'unresolved disarmament issues' and were working on defining these and outlining what was expected of Iraq on each. With this methodical, analytical approach, I could see that if Iraq ever agreed to let inspectors back in the country, there could possibly be a way forward and the crippling sanctions on the country could be lifted.

Coincidentally, while I was in Canberra a few months earlier, I had penned my own ideas on the path forward for Iraq. I had given copies of 'A Strategic Plan for UNMOVIC' to the Department of Foreign Affairs and the Department of Defence, but neither seemed interested, and I imagine that it was immediately archived, or discarded. I wondered whether I should give a copy to Blix – would he see it as the height of arrogance, telling him what he should be doing?

My ideas were a little different to Blix's, but there was also much overlap. My plan took the process he had started one step further, in that it proposed that the significance of each unresolved issue should be considered. For example, if a biological agent had, with time, deteriorated to become largely ineffective, although the issue may not be resolved, it could safely be put aside.

Sitting in Blix's office, listening to his approach on dealing with Iraq, I took the plunge and gave him my paper, with apologies for the implication that I was telling him how he might do his job. To my surprise, he handed me a copy of an unrelated study done by one of his staff. We sat quietly for a few minutes, each reading the other's work. Eventually he looked up and said, 'I like your paper. What do you think of ours?'

I told him, as diplomatically as possible, that I could see some problems with 'his' paper and explained briefly what they were.

He responded with, 'That's exactly what I thought. Would you go and discuss this with the author?'

I was astonished that he had asked me to tell one of his staff where I thought he had gone wrong, though I liked his direct approach to problem-solving. Nevertheless, I declined.

Jan and I stayed in New York for a few more days, enjoying this magnificent city that we had both come to know quite well. Before we left, we were invited to lunch by Judith Miller, a journalist from *The New York Times*.

I had first met Judith a few years earlier, shortly after Iraq had confessed to a biological warfare program. Rolf Ekéus thought that it would be a good idea to gain some publicity for UNSCOM and authorised the Gang of Four to cooperate with her for an article. So on 26 February 1998, I found myself on the front page of *The New York Times*, explaining how 17 tonnes of missing bacterial growth media led to the uncovering of Iraq's hidden program. As an intelligence officer, the last thing I welcomed was publicity, but as far as Judith and the world were concerned, I was just a weapons inspector with the United Nations. So under this guise, I accepted it.

Judith and I kept in touch from time to time, so the lunch invite was not unexpected. What was unexpected is that over lunch, she handed me a short document containing raw intelligence on Iraq's biological weapons program. Although it was declassified and all the intelligence markers had been removed, I could tell that it had once been a CIA document. On the top were the words *Not Finally Evaluated Intelligence*, suggesting that the CIA had little further interest in this so-called intelligence.

She told me that a lot of former intelligence material had now been released and was available on the internet. Most of this, she acknowledged, was rubbish, but this piece struck her as containing new information. 'Rod, what I'd really like to know is, what do you make of it? Is it genuine?'

I scanned the document quickly, took another sip of my wine, sat back and gave her my considered view. 'Well, there's nothing new here. It's just another piece of junk.'

Document X, as we'll call it, referred to hidden biological warheads and bombs at various sites in Iraq, and gave the numbers and the codes that Iraq used for anthrax and other biological agents. But the Gang of Four had uncovered this information, so to me now, over a rather nice lunch, there seemed nothing particularly remarkable. Judith seemed disappointed; this was not going to be the basis for another headline.

That afternoon, as Jan and I headed back to Washington on the Metroliner, I took Document X out to help pass the time on a drab winter's day. Suddenly I forgot where I was. What had caught my attention was the date of the information: August 1991.

In August 1991, Iraq was denying that it ever had a biological weapons program, and very few Iraqis would have known of its existence. Even among those in the know, only a handful of individuals might be aware of where missile warheads and bombs filled with anthrax and other agents would be hidden from the prying eyes of UN weapons inspectors. The source of this raw information clearly had great access to highly sensitive information.

The detail in Document X was good, down to the exact numbers. But there was one bit that was new to me. Logically, if everything else was true, this must also be.

The new information referred to containers of biological agent hidden near 'Electronic Warfare Unit 114', which I had never heard of. The source explained:

> STORED NEAR THE MILITARY'S ELECTRONIC WARFARE UNIT 114 INSIDE A PRE-FABRICATED BUILDING ARE 23 ONE-METER CONTAINERS OF AGENT A, B AND C. SEVENTY-NINE CONTAINERS OF AGENT C ARE ALSO STORED IN THIS BUILDING.

I knew what biological agents the Iraqi codes A, B and C referred to – for example, agent B was anthrax. I also was very familiar with Iraq's 'ONE METER CONTAINERS' and their actual capacity. I started scribbling some numbers on the corner of *The New York Times*. If my calculation was correct, Iraq had produced significantly more anthrax than it had admitted to. Perhaps this explained the still-missing bacterial growth media. What's more, it appeared that the entire Iraqi stockpile of biological warfare agents had been tucked away in 1991 at some location the Gang of Four had no knowledge of. Perhaps it was still there?

Agents A and C did not concern me much, as after ten years, they would probably have degraded. Anthrax was a different matter. It had a lifespan of a 100 years, particularly as Iraq had found a way of stabilising it. This therefore was a deadly serious matter. I could see now that Document X was a significant find, and proof that Iraq had not come clean.

I was annoyed with myself for being so dismissive of Document X when Judith had handed it to me. As a former director of intelligence, I should have readily identified its significance. Perhaps that second glass of wine had fuddled my brain. At the same time, I was pleased that I had dismissed it then, because it would have been headlines in the next day's paper. Better to keep it secret and use it to elicit confessions from the Iraqis if the opportunity arose.

I wanted to see whether the CIA had any more information from this source. I phoned one of my agency contacts – let's call him Henry Staples – and suggested we have coffee at a café I knew in Georgetown. We sat at a corner table where we would not be overheard and could keep our eyes on the other patrons. There was probably no need for the cloak-and-dagger, but it was part of the tradecraft for both of us, a habit that was hard to shake.

I told Henry what I had discovered on the train journey and why I thought that we might now have evidence of Iraqi duplicity over its biological weapons program. It took a moment or two before the light went on and he saw how damning this could be for Iraq. Up to now we only had suspicions that Iraq had not declared everything, but here was hard evidence. It certainly required some explaining.

I asked whether he would find out if the source was still available, and if there were any more reports by him or her. I recognised that providing me with this information might cause some problems for Henry. I was no longer employed by DIO or the UN, and no longer held any security clearances. On the other hand, I pointed out to him, without me he would have nothing – I still had not handed over a copy of Document X. Henry acknowledged that the document had somehow been overlooked by his agency and promised to give me what he could. In the intelligence world, the rules sometimes have to be flexible.

A couple of days later, I received a call from Hans Blix, who asked if I would be interested in joining his staff as his special advisor. He explained that while he wanted people with fresh ideas, he also thought this needed to be balanced with experience. I was still not sure whether I wanted to be part of his outfit. While I admired his approach, it all seemed rather academic unless the inspectors could get back into Iraq. On the other hand, Document X might prove useful if I was working for the United Nations. I thanked Blix for the generous offer and said I would consider it.

I had commitments in Australia, not the least to report back to the parliamentary committee on the Middle East. I decided to return via the United Kingdom. Jan would meet me at Heathrow for the last leg of the journey. Thanks to all the frequent flyer miles I had accumulated, I flew at twice the speed of sound on a British Airways Concorde from New York to London, and Jan, following in a lumbering Boeing 747, eventually caught up with me a few hours later.

I was keen to see David Kelly to talk to him about UNMOVIC and Blix's offer of a senior position. Jan and I stayed with David for a couple of days at his old farmhouse near Oxford. In this beautiful and peaceful part of England, the problems of Iraq and the politics of the United Nations, away in New York, seemed to belong to another time. Nevertheless, we talked for a day and a half on the subject while Jan and Janice, David's wife, went into town to shop.

David agreed with Blix on one thing: the lack of experienced inspectors in UNMOVIC was a major problem. 'You have to remember,' he said, 'that the same people in Iraq have been dealing with these issues since 1991. They know all the tricks and will run rings round UNMOVIC inspectors.'

David argued that whatever we thought of Blix's outfit, it would surely do better with one of the old guard in their ranks. I was mulling over this when his phone rang. On the other end was Blix's head of administration. She asked David if he happened to know where I was. Either this was fate, or UNMOVIC had a better intelligence service than the CIA.

Swayed by David's logic, I agreed I would take up a contract as Blix's special advisor, but only for four months. If the job proved to be pointless, at least I wouldn't have wasted too much of my time. I also thought this would be an ideal opportunity to discuss Document X with UNMOVIC staff, and perhaps bring in Henry, with whatever he had managed to dig out of the CIA system. I was beginning to warm to the opportunities of the role.

I started work with UNMOVIC in May 2001. After leaving UNSCOM, I didn't think that I would ever again become closely involved with Iraq and its weapons of mass destruction, but here I was. And so was Hamish. He had taken up the job of training would-be inspectors on what they were to face if they ever got to enter Iraq. In typical Hamish fashion, he designed inspection exercises at some old factory sites in New Jersey to put the 'inspectors' through their paces. He would hide fake 'biological bombs' in the factory while he would play an obstructive Iraqi official. It was like a game of hide-and-seek but with much higher stakes.

As Hans Blix's special advisor, I found myself in his office almost every day explaining technical matters or discussing what needed to go in the regular reports that the Security Council demanded, even mulling over staff problems. Blix was an easy person to work with, and we had similar views on many matters. Our relationship was also helped by a shared sense of humour.

But most of my time was spent helping the staff, who were working on the unresolved disarmament issues. Many of the fresh faces found it challenging work and struggled to cope with the vast database of over a million pages of information that UNSCOM had built up over the years. As a former DIO intelligence analyst, this was my bread and butter, and I guided them to work their way slowly through the maze.

Of course, I had not forgotten Document X. Eventually Henry and some of his CIA colleagues turned up at UNMOVIC, to brief a select few staff on the document and what else they had found in their database. At that stage I only wanted those who could be trusted to have this information, as any leak to the media might compromise its utility. I was also concerned that the Iraqi source of the intelligence could be placed at deadly risk if the information became public. The CIA shared this concern, and Document X had been quietly pulled from the internet.

Disappointingly, Henry could only add a few extra snippets to what I already knew. But even this was a help, and I took it upon myself to write an analysis of Document X to show to Blix later in the year.

My contract ended in early September 2001, but I had agreed to return in October. With Jan in Washington and me in New York, weekends had been spent commuting between the two cities. We came to know just about every house along the train line. It was all part of the rather strange jobs we found ourselves in. But it was good to spend a little time together in the one place before I headed home to give a couple of presentations at various institutes. What I could not have anticipated is that during my short departure the world would change dramatically.

On 11 September 2001, al-Qaeda terrorists flew passenger jets into the twin towers in New York. 9/11 went down as a date infamous in history. Jan called me from Washington and told me to turn on the television. She said that a plane had just crashed into one of the towers of the World Trade Center, and there was confusion over whether this was an accident or deliberate. When the second plane hit, there was no doubt that this was an act of terrorism. ASIO was now on high alert.

Jan later filled me in on her experience in Washington. Shortly before calling me, she had been on the phone to one of her contacts in the CIA. In the Embassy, the ASIO office was monitoring the unfolding incident on television, and her CIA contact, hearing the background noise, asked her what she was doing. Jan simply told her that they were watching the telly. Her contact laughed, oblivious of the unfolding events until Jan explained and the officer, shocked, immediately ended the call. It seems even they did not know what was happening.

Chaos soon came to the city of Washington, too, when another plane hit the Pentagon. At the time, Australia's prime minister, John Howard, was giving a press conference in his hotel, the Willard, close to the White House. He was immediately bundled up by the US Secret Service and taken to the Australian Embassy, just a short distance away. There he was put in the carpenter's room in the sub-basement, which is below the basement carpark and as deep and secure a hidey-hole as the Embassy has. As the Embassy gradually closed up for the night, just a few staff were left on duty, including Jan's intelligence cell, which continued to monitor developments late into the evening. She therefore found herself trotting down the stairs from time to time to the carpenter's workshop to serve coffee and Tim Tams to John Howard, until he too was evacuated.

I returned to a very different New York just after 9/11. Even getting into UN headquarters was now difficult, with tight security and the streets surrounding the iconic building closed off by dump trucks laden with sand to provide an impenetrable barrier to any vehicle driven by would-be suicide bombers. The mood in the streets was sombre, mixed with a dash of fear. It was as if the heart of the city had been ripped out.

I wasn't sure what implications the events of 9/11 might have on Iraq, but I thought it would be prudent to finish my assessment of

Document X. I needed to be sure that all my assumptions and calculations could be justified, so that my conclusions could withstand the deepest scrutiny. At the same time, I needed to make it decipherable to a non-technical audience.

I handed my findings to Blix at the end of December, and he invited me to discuss them with him on 3 January 2002. He understood and accepted my conclusions, and they clearly disturbed him. 'How do we handle this, Rod?'

To me the answer seemed obvious: the UN Security Council needed to be informed immediately. This was not so obvious to him. An announcement that we had overwhelming evidence Iraq had potentially hidden stockpiles of anthrax would be explosive, especially in the current political climate.

I pointed out that although the evidence indicated that Iraq had at one time hidden anthrax stockpiles from inspectors and never declared this to us, we did not know if they still had it. For all we knew, Iraq could have destroyed it later, along with other agents they claimed to have dispensed with. The wording I had used in my assessment was cautious: 'The ultimate fate of the anthrax is unknown.' Blix suggested a better conclusion would be, 'There must be a strong presumption that the anthrax still exists.' It was surprisingly tough language from the usually circumspect Blix, but the logic was inescapable, and I agreed to the change.

Blix decided that we needed to discuss where to go from here with senior staff, and a meeting was held a few days later in his office. I argued that if we did not tell the Council now, it would look like a cover-up. Others argued that we should wait until the political climate had cooled a bit; publishing my report now might make us seem a tool of the United States. Blix's executive assistant summed it up: 'Damned if we do, and damned if we don't.'

In the end, Blix, with his lawyer's hat on, decided there was nothing in UNMOVIC's mandate that required us to report it immediately. He thought that our best option was to include it in the list of unresolved disarmament issues and publish it in a couple of months, when analysis of these issues had been completed. But he did take my advice, and instructed that my paper on Document X not be circulated to staff outside the close leadership group.

The timing for the release of my analysis on Document X, however, only got worse. Jan and I took a short holiday to San Francisco at the end of January 2002, and before we went out to dinner that first night, we listened to President George W. Bush's State of the Union address. Given the continued political tension in the United States, it promised to be dynamic, but even I was surprised at what he had to say.

Bush began: 'Our nation is at war … and the civilised world faces unprecedented dangers.'

He went on to single out Iraq as one of the great threats facing the United States. 'Iraq continues to flaunt its hostility toward America and to support terror. The Iraqi regime has plotted to develop anthrax and nerve gas and nuclear weapons for over a decade. This is a regime that has already used poison gas to murder thousands of its own citizens, leaving the bodies of mothers huddled over their dead children. This is a regime that agreed to international inspections, then kicked out the inspectors. This is a regime that has something to hide from the civilised world. States like these, and their terrorist allies, constitute an axis of evil, arming to threaten the peace of the world. By seeking weapons of mass destruction, these regimes pose a grave and growing danger.'

Why had Iraq been singled out? The terrorists who had wrought such havoc in New York and Washington had nothing to do with Iraq. In fact, Saddam Hussein had distanced his regime from al-Qaeda; they were his enemies, too. I also wondered what was behind his claim that Iraq 'has something to hide from the civilised world'. Could this be an oblique reference to the information from Document X? Did the US president know about it?

The phrasing that I had most trouble with, though, was that Iraq posed 'a grave and growing danger'. I thought it more than possible that Iraq had hidden some relatively small quantities of anthrax and other agents, but it did not have the means to deliver these materials much beyond its own borders. After the Gulf War, Iraq had been left with only a few ageing bomber aircraft, and its once impressive missile force had all but been destroyed. Under the sanctions, it had no way to rebuild them.

I felt sure that Bush's statements on Iraq would have come as a surprise to the CIA and other US intelligence agencies. As far as my own US intelligence contacts were concerned, Iraq was a backwater. I was certain they did not see Iraq as 'flaunting its hostility towards America' and 'a grave and growing danger'. If I was right,

Bush's pronouncements were not based on any intelligence reports, but were purely political statements.

Over dinner, Jan and I discussed what this might mean for Iraq. Was it possible that the United States might re-start the Gulf War? Surely not?! We also discussed what the UN's role might be in all of this. I feared that, one way or another, we would be dragged in to support Bush's political agenda.

Bush's intentions towards Iraq became sharper a couple of months later, when he announced: 'In preventing the spread of weapons of mass destruction, there is no margin for error, and no chance to learn from mistakes. Our coalition must act deliberately, but inaction is not an option.'

Now it was clear that he envisaged some sort of action, and I assumed this did not mean another UN resolution. I believed he was firmly set on the path to war with Iraq from here – if he hadn't been before. This of course made the publication of my findings on Document X even more problematic. It was one thing for the United States to accuse Iraq of hiding weapons of mass destruction, but quite another for the supposedly unbiased United Nations to do so. And anything we did say, however carefully expressed, would only be used by US leadership to justify aggression towards Iraq.

By the end of April 2002, the assessment of the unresolved disarmament issues was complete. We had narrowed the list down from more than 100 issues to just twenty-nine, but almost all were relatively minor. For example, the number of containers that Iraq had manufactured for storing biological agent: did it really matter whether it was twenty or twenty-five? The missing anthrax was another matter altogether. We had proof in Document X that the Iraqis had made more than they had admitted to and that they had hidden it from inspectors – and they could still be hiding it. I had calculated that at least 3000 litres of concentrated anthrax were unaccounted for. This was a significant amount, but in my view it was not enough to go to war over. It was obvious, however, that Bush would see it differently.

Blix was now adamant that we could not give our assessments to the Security Council – it would be like adding petrol to a fire. I was glad it was he, not me, who had to make the decisions in this dilemma. There was not going to be a good time to reveal our findings in the near future, but we faced accusations of a cover-up if we published too late.

As 2002 wore on, the language from the Bush administration on Iraq became even more aggressive. As I celebrated my birthday over dinner with Jan on 8 July, we pondered Bush's latest missive: 'A stated policy of this government is to have regime change. And it hasn't changed. And we'll use all tools at our disposal to do so.'

If we weren't already convinced that war was coming, this was the clincher.

I was still not entirely clear on Bush's political agenda. If the United States pitted its military might against Iraq, regime change could quite likely be the messy outcome. What then? Was America going to occupy Iraq, or attempt to put in a puppet government? And why? It could not be because the Bush government feared a few thousand litres of anthrax or whatever else Iraq might have squirrelled away; that just didn't make sense.

I wondered what my CIA colleagues were making of all this. At the beginning of the year, Iraq was not considered a serious threat to the United States. Were the politics now driving them to reassess this?

Pronouncements on Iraq from the Bush regime were now coming thick and fast, with the US secretary of defence, Donald Rumsfeld, and the vice-president, Dick Cheney, adding to the gaggle. Saddam Hussein, the target of much of this rhetoric, was beginning to take note. He sent senior delegations to New York to talk to Blix about the possibility of renewing inspections. Although I was his special advisor, Blix decided that I should not be part of these talks because, he argued, given my previous contretemps with some members of the Iraqi delegations, my presence might be misinterpreted. Knowing that General Amer Rashid would be among the delegations, I could see his point, but was nevertheless disappointed.

As I had envisaged, the United Nations was getting dragged into this mess. Bush addressed the Security Council on 12 September, just after the first anniversary of 9/11. As expected, it was an aggressive speech. He spoke of the threat Iraq posed to world peace because of its weapons of mass destruction, particularly its biological weapons: 'UN inspectors believe Iraq has produced two to four times the amount of biological agents it declared, and has failed to account for more than three metric tons of material that could be used to produce biological weapons.'

This was not what we believed at all! Based on Document X, I believed that they may have had 25 per cent more agent than declared. I wondered where his figures had come from. I could not accept what he said next: 'Saddam Hussein's regime is a grave and gathering danger. To suggest otherwise is to hope against the evidence. To assume this regime's good faith is to bet the lives of millions and the peace of the world in a reckless gamble. And this is a risk we must not take.'

He went on: 'Will the United Nations serve the purpose of its founding, or will it be irrelevant?'

I felt that we had already become irrelevant. The United States was on a path to war with Iraq. Anything we said would either be ignored or used to bolster the US case.

About a week after Bush's speech to the Council, Iraq agreed to the 'unconditional' return of weapons inspectors, but this seemed anti-climactic. Inspections were irrelevant when Bush was demanding regime change.

It was not long before the United Kingdom showed its colours, too. At the end of September, the Blair government published an assessment of Iraq's weapons of mass destruction capabilities in a document that came to be known as The Dossier. This was allegedly based on British intelligence, but seemed to parrot what Bush had been telling the Security Council. After three years spent as the Australian intelligence liaison officer in London, I found it hard to believe that my UK colleagues had made a 180-degree turn in their assessments of Iraq.

I discussed The Dossier with Blix. Had the Brits suddenly found a bunch of new sources that would make the UN investigations on Iraq over the past decade obsolete? It seemed unlikely.

I prepared a long list of questions on The Dossier, querying the startling new information the Brits implied they had. UNMOVIC had a special office innocently named 'Outside Information Sources'. It was actually an intelligence unit run by a former deputy director of the Canadian Secret Intelligence Service, and access to its information was tightly held. In fact, many of the inspectors in UNMOVIC were probably not even aware of its existence. The head of Outside Information Sources undertook to liaise with British intelligence to see if she could elicit some answers, but neither of us were very hopeful of a reply. We both suspected The Dossier was more hype than reality.

As 2002 neared its end, pressure on Iraq from the United States and United Kingdom mounted. Throughout the year they had been pushing the Security Council for a new resolution on Iraq. I had seen drafts; it was by far the toughest resolution I had ever seen. It required Iraq to declare all the weapons that Bush and Blair claimed Iraq had hidden. Failure to do so would result in immediate military action. A slightly amended version of this resolution was unanimously passed by the Council on 8 November 2002.

The preamble set the tone for what was to come. It highlighted the threat that Iraq posed 'to international peace and security'. Iraq had 'a final opportunity to comply with its disarmament obligations', and if it did not, it would 'face serious consequences'. Exactly what 'serious consequences' meant was open to interpretation, but at least it had been toned down from drafts that authorised 'all necessary means' – that is, automatic military action.

I could immediately see the dilemma facing Iraq and, for that matter, UNMOVIC. The United States and United Kingdom were accusing Iraq of having capabilities that we, UNMOVIC, had no knowledge of. I strongly suspected that Iraq too had no knowledge of these capabilities, because it was all hype. What, then, was Iraq to do? If it did not possess the weapons it had been accused of hiding, compliance would be impossible.

It was true that UNMOVIC had identified a number of issues, such as the missing anthrax, that remained unresolved. But even if Iraq could satisfy us on these, it would go nowhere near placating the United States and United Kingdom on matters they believed were posing a threat to 'international peace and security'. Iraq was now well and truly cooked!

Blix, and by association UNMOVIC, now came under pressure from the United States. In an effort to discredit him, the US government conducted an investigation into Blix's background. While nothing untoward was uncovered, there was sufficient in the unresolved disarmament issues to raise eyebrows. The US media jumped on the bandwagon, probably assisted by leaks from the CIA. *The Washington Times* reported:

> US intelligence agencies have told UN weapons inspectors that Iraq has hidden 7,000 liters of anthrax, but chief inspector

> Hans Blix never reported the information to the U.N. Security Council … The failure to inform the council has raised questions about whether Mr. Blix will report accurately on anticipated Iraqi obstruction of weapons inspections … The failure to alert the Security Council to the anthrax stockpile has upset some Bush administration officials, who said the information might have helped persuade some members of the council to support tougher U. S. action.

The figure cited was more than double what I had calculated from Document X, but otherwise the accusation was essentially correct. We had covered up important information that we had been sitting on since the beginning of the year, and as Blix's advisor I felt it more than unfortunate that he had ignored my advice not to publish earlier. By now, though, it hardly mattered; we had become irrelevant.

Judgement day was coming for Iraq. Under the UN resolution, Iraq was required to declare, in detail, everything about its weapons of mass destruction programs and the so-called missing weapons.

Iraq's response to the resolution was delivered by Iraqi officials to Blix's office at 8.05 pm on Sunday, 8 December 2002, under the gaze of the international press. Blix had asked a few senior staff to be there to receive it. It was my job, as the only technical person in this group, to have a quick look through to see if I could spot anything significantly new that might point to the existence of hidden weapons.

The declaration was 12,000 pages, but after more than ten years of looking at Iraqi declarations, I could tell fairly quickly that there was nothing substantially new, just some bits presented slightly differently. By 11 pm that evening, I gave my initial assessment to Blix and the others. We all were aware of the consequences: there would be nothing now to stop the United States and the United Kingdom from going to war over this.

In the following weeks, I coordinated a more thorough analysis of the Iraqi declaration with teams of UNMOVIC weapons experts, poring over tables, diagrams and text. Essentially, they came to the same conclusion I had. We now had to report our findings to the Security Council. Blix gave me the job of drafting the technical summary while he drafted the political aspects, including comment on Iraqi cooperation and truthfulness. As Sweden's former foreign minister, he was more than equipped to steer through the thorny issues as the Council decided what to do in the face of approaching war.

The brief to the Council was scheduled for the end of January 2003. A couple of days before, Blix invited me into his office to see what I had drafted and to discuss what he was going to tell the council. I sat down and Blix said, with a grin on his face, 'You show me yours and I'll show you mine.' Of course, he meant the drafts. After a bit of massaging of the language, we reached a final version. I felt that we had the balance right. I thought it crucial that we told it as it was. For the first time, we would be revealing to the council what we had learned from Document X.

I would have liked to put into the draft that although we believed there was 'missing' anthrax and possibly other missing materials, including nerve gas, none of these items justified military action: Iraq was not a threat to the world. I knew, however, that to tell the Council this was to go well beyond our mandate. And Blix, as an international lawyer, was conscious of our legal position and would not have had it anyway. In any case, no matter how we couched our assessments, war seemed inevitable.

At 10.30 am on 27 January 2003, Blix briefed the Council. The information that everyone had been waiting for took about five minutes to deliver.

'One might have expected that in preparing the declaration, Iraq would have tried to respond to, clarify and submit supporting evidence regarding the many open disarmament issues, which the Iraqi side should be familiar with,' Blix began. These 'open disarmament issues', he said, 'deserve to be taken seriously by Iraq rather than being brushed aside as evil machinations of UNSCOM. Regrettably, the 12,000 page declaration, most of which is a reprint of earlier documents, does not seem to contain any new evidence that would eliminate the questions or reduce their number.'

If the Council was waiting on words that might decide whether military action was necessary, these few sentences were it. But, as we all knew, two member-states of the Council had already made up their minds.

Then Blix came to the bit I had written about my findings on Document X: 'There are strong indications that Iraq produced more anthrax than it declared, and that at least some of this was retained after the declared destruction date. It might still exist. Either it should be found and be destroyed under UNMOVIC supervision, or else convincing evidence should be produced to show that it was, indeed, destroyed in 1991.'

We had toned down Blix's earlier phrasing 'there must be a strong presumption that the anthrax still exists'. Instead, the possibility that Iraq might have destroyed it, along with the other anthrax, sometime during 1991 was floated. We had written it as we saw it. I felt that to do anything less would have been dishonest.

As expected, both the United States and the United Kingdom used Blix's report to justify their stance on Iraq. The US ambassador to the United Nations, John D. Negroponte, announced: 'The declaration was a fundamental test of cooperation and intent, and Iraq failed it resoundingly.' The UK foreign secretary, Jack Straw, continued the theme, describing Blix's report as 'damning and disturbing' and adding that it showed a 'consistent pattern of concealment and deceit' by Iraq.

My guess is that if we had tried to moderate the language, we would have been accused of misleading the Security Council. Blix, too, must have anticipated the US and UK response, but even so he was disturbed by it. I sensed that when war came, he might see himself as somehow a promulgator. He was a man of peace trapped in a conundrum.

A week later, the US Secretary of State, Colin Powell, gave the US assessment on Iraq to the Security Council. Blix and Kofi Annan, the UN secretary-general, sat at one end of the Council chamber while Powell, backed by the director of the CIA, George Tenet, sat at the other. Despite being Blix's special advisor, I was only allowed to watch the proceedings on closed-circuit television.

There was some predictability about Powell's presentation, but there were also surprises. Powell opened by quoting Blix's words to the council of a few days before: 'As Dr Blix reported to this council on January 27, quote, "Iraq appears not to have come to a genuine acceptance, not even today, of the disarmament which was demanded of it", unquote.' I could see Blix wince at these lines.

Powell went on to outline the evidence the United States had of Iraq's hidden capabilities. Unusually for such a presentation, he revealed some of the intelligence the United States possessed to back his claims, and for greater impact projected slides onto a large screen to illustrate his points. He played snippets of intercepted Iraqi communications that suggested Iraq was hiding chemical weapons. He showed satellite pictures of an ammunition depot, Al Mussayib, where the CIA believed these weapons were hidden.

On nuclear weapons, Powell showed pictures of aluminium tubes that the Iraq defence establishment had been caught importing despite the sanctions. He claimed the tubes were of such a particular specification they could only be for one purpose, and that was enriching uranium. This was clear evidence, he said, that Iraq had not abandoned its nuclear weapons program.

Perhaps most convincing was his testimony on biological weapons. The United States had several sources, he said, that reported Iraq had developed a mobile anthrax production facility. They even had on record one individual, a chemical engineer, who had helped to construct such a biological plant. He showed an artist's impression of what the facility looked like, based on this source's reporting. It consisted of three semi-trailers, each holding part of the plant. The idea was that the trailers would scurry around the country, thereby keeping out of sight of UN inspectors' prying eyes.

This last piece of intelligence was not as ridiculous as it may have sounded. Iraq had acknowledged to the Gang of Four that mobile biological facilities had been considered, but claimed that they posed technical challenges not easily solved. Because of this, they said, the concept was abandoned and the facility at Al Hakam was constructed instead.

I was not sure what to make of the revelations. It contradicted what the UN inspectors understood about Iraq's weapons programs. At the same time, it appeared that the CIA had some good sources. The questions were, how reliable were the sources, what collateral intelligence was there to support the information and, perhaps most importantly, how good was the analysis of the intelligence that had been obtained? All too frequently as a director of intelligence I had seen analysts get carried away with bits of information they had put together to form an erroneous picture. Unpleasant memories of the Yellow Rain debacle flashed into my mind.

After discussing Powell's presentation with Blix, I went again to UNMOVIC's Outside Information Sources office, this time with a series of questions for the CIA. We did not expect much of a response from the Americans, and we were not wrong. I thought

I might never learn the answers to the questions I had about why Powell believed what he did. It turned out I was wrong, but it would take almost another year before I discovered the truth.

We all now waited for the ‘serious consequences’ Iraq had been promised to play out.

CHAPTER 10

CAMP SLAYER

'That men do not learn much from the lessons of history is the most important of all the lessons of history.'

Aldous Huxley

By early March 2003, there was little doubt that a war on Iraq would start soon. I even received a phone call in my UNMOVIC office from a senior CIA officer, saying that war was inevitable. Assuming that the United States was successful in overturning the Iraqi regime, he asked carefully, would I like to join the post-war effort to help locate the missing weapons that Colin Powell had briefed the Security Council on?

The CIA had just made me an offer I could not refuse.

I told Blix about the offer. I was still his special advisor – though not for much longer. My contract was coming to an end and, despite his offer to extend it, I felt there was little point in staying with UNSCOM if there was a war. The United Nations had become collateral damage and was now irrelevant as far as Iraq's weapons of mass destruction were concerned. Blix reluctantly accepted the situation, and even joked good-humouredly, 'So, you will be part of the Coalition of Willing Inspectors, then.'

The Coalition of the Willing, which included the United States, the United Kingdom and Australia, entered into conflict with Iraq on 19 March 2003. Under the moniker 'Operation Iraqi Freedom', a massive bombing campaign on Baghdadi targets was launched. I wondered about the naming of the operation. What was Iraq being freed from? Presumably it referred to the elimination of the Saddam regime and its replacement with something more benign, perhaps a US presence. But it seemed a curious choice when the justification for the war was Iraq's weapons of mass destruction and the alleged threat they posed to world peace.

I returned to Australia at the end of March. Jan's posting to Washington had ended a few months before, so it was good to be back together in peaceful Australia, away from the politics and frenetic pace of work in the United Nations. I was now unemployed again, but looked forward to taking up the CIA offer when the position had been formalised, after the war.

Depending on your point of view, and on the definition of the 'end of hostilities', the war did not last long. According to President Bush, it was 'Mission Accomplished' on 1 May 2003. But it seems to me that the war has continued in various forms right up to the present day.

I should have guessed that anything as politically charged as finding weapons of mass destruction, thereby justifying the rationale for going to war, would not be straightforward. Initially the US military took it on themselves to find Iraq's 'hidden' weapons, and set up a group known as the 75th Exploitation Task Force. They had little expertise in weapons of mass destruction, but their view was that since the military had to face the dangers of war, it should be they who came home with the trophies. After what Powell had told the UN Security Council, surely the hidden weapons would not be hard to find?

When that was not so, there were squabbles in Washington over which organisation should take on the task. Not surprisingly, the CIA eventually won. However, although it was to lead the search, it was required to involve other intelligence agencies to assist with the task. In the end, the CIA grudgingly invited a few personnel from about ten agencies, including the US Treasury, the Los Alamos nuclear laboratory and the National Security Agency, as well as the usual suspects from the DIA and the FBI. To complete the set, a few experts from the United Kingdom and Australia would also be invited, with the idea that this would 'internationalise' the effort.

This new organisation would be under the control of the CIA's director, George Tenet, and be known as the Iraq Survey Group, ISG. To me the name sounded like we were a cartography mission, but perhaps it was designed to mislead, to put outsiders off the scent that this was a CIA operation.

I received my invitation to join the ISG through the Australian bureaucracy, rather than directly from the CIA. Accordingly, I was offered a very bureaucratic contract. It stipulated that I would be employed as a 'non-ongoing' public servant (whatever that meant) at a relatively junior level, and I would have a three-month probation period, during which I could be terminated if I did not perform to the expected standard. I declined the contract on principle. Not only did it not reflect my expertise in these matters, it did not seem to take into account the dangers of the job. I would have gone for no pay at all, but not under the conditions offered. I thought perhaps the Australian Department of Defence, which had drafted the contract, did not really want to employ me – or maybe it was simply that I had been away too long, and now no one knew me.

After a month, the deputy director of the CIA, John McLaughlin, asked the Australian minister of defence, who was visiting Washington, why I had not signed on to the ISG yet. McLaughlin explained that he wanted me as the special advisor to David Kay, the head of the group, and since work would start in late June, this was becoming urgent.

With the minister's backing, I could now set my own terms and conditions of employment. However, the bureaucratic wheels still turned slowly. First, I had to go through a new vetting process to regain my Top Secret security clearances. At the interview, I was asked whether I had ever come into contact with overseas intelligence officers. If I had, I might somehow be compromised, I was told, and the granting of security clearances would be out of the question. 'Of course I've come into contact with foreign intelligence agents,' I answered. At the United Nations, I explained, I had had regular contact with many intelligence agencies, such as the KGB, Mossad and whatever the Chinese foreign bureau called itself. This caused the clearance officers a bit of scurrying to see if this hiccup could be overcome.

Then, of course, there was a medical check and a series of injections to protect me from the usual diseases, and anthrax and rabies, among other things. Finally, I was sent off to the Holsworthy Barracks, where I joined a military team for a week's training on the hazards I might face in Iraq. This included putting on a respirator, entering a 'gas chamber' filled with tear gas and performing various tasks inside. It also included Army-type exercises such as crawling through a minefield, probing the earth to locate unexploded landmines. I hoped this was a skill I would not need on my return to Iraq.

I passed all the tests and was ready to go – after a briefing at Defence headquarters in Canberra, where my responsibilities in Iraq were explained to me. Strangely, it was emphasised that although the contract was with the Australian Department of Defence, I was not working for the Australian government but for the CIA. I had no problem with this, except I did wonder where my loyalties should lie: I was Australian, and my wages were being paid by the Australian taxpayer, after all. But now I was to become a CIA official, of a kind.

I assumed that the other members of the Gang of Four would be joining me in the hunt for Iraq's missing weapons, and we could finally close this chapter as a team. However, Dick, at sixty-nine, was deemed too old for the rigours of Iraq and had been crossed off the US list. Curiously, the age limit had been set at sixty-eight. Hamish gave me a call and told me he would soon be heading off to Iraq. David, too, would be working with the ISG, Hamish said: in fact, the

UK government had tried to send him to Iraq already, in May, on a sort of reconnaissance mission that would help in planning how to tackle the hunt. Unfortunately, there had been some misunderstanding – he got as far as Kuwait and, for some reason, could not travel on to Baghdad and returned home. There was some sort of parliamentary inquiry that David was involved in, Hamish said, so his official joining of the ISG might be delayed. While I would miss the presence of Dick in our team, I thought that three out of four wasn't bad.

I was soon to learn that only two of the Gang of Four would return to Iraq. I woke early on 19 July 2003 and turned on the radio. The first item on ABC News was the tragic death of David Kelly. His body had been found in the woods, not far from his home. Suicide was suspected.

I could hardly believe what I'd heard. David was a close colleague and a friend. He had only been fifty-nine, with a lot of living ahead. In fact, he had told me when we last met that when all the Iraq nonsense was over, he had plans to work in the United States as an academic. David seemed like one of the last people you would expect to commit suicide. I wondered whether General Amer Rashid had delivered David a death threat similar to the one he had whispered to me. Could that possibly be an explanation?

Over the next few weeks I was to learn of the events leading up to David's death. In the United Kingdom, there had been a leak of information over the validity of The Dossier on Iraq's weapons of mass destruction. Given the nature of the information leaked, David had been a suspect. He had denied to a parliamentary committee that he was the source, although he did acknowledge that he had spoken to some journalists in the course of his job. The press staked out his house and he found himself under extreme pressure, not only from the media, but also from the parliamentary committee itself, which was beginning to question if it had been told the truth. David's integrity, and possibly his career, was under threat.

Eventually I came to accept that, given the dark place David found himself in, he probably did take his own life. Whatever the circumstances of his death, the sadness was made all the greater by the realisation that I would not be meeting up with him again when I returned to Iraq.

* * *

There was one thing I was looking forward to in Iraq: being David Kay's special advisor. I had met him only once, briefly, back in my GATEWAY days, when his team was busy smuggling nuclear documents out of Baghdad. He was not CIA, so was perhaps an unusual choice to head a CIA operation, but his credentials were impeccable. He was a former chief inspector with the International Atomic Energy Agency, a man of a tough, determined nature who would take no nonsense from the Iraqis. Perhaps most importantly, he had an unshakeable belief that there were illegal weapons hidden somewhere in Iraq. The CIA were confident that he would find them.

With all the delays, training and preparation in Australia, Jan and I did not say our goodbyes until early December 2003. Getting to Baghdad was not quite as easy as I thought. Travelling on a diplomatic passport again, like any good spy, my first port was Kuwait. I was met there by an Australian Army major who whisked me away to the giant US military base of Camp Doha, where I was told I might have to wait a week or so until an Australian Hercules transport plane could fly me into Baghdad.

Impatient to start the job, the following day I wangled my way onto a British military flight that took off at night. It stopped briefly at the southern Iraqi port of Basra and arrived in the relative security of darkness at the so-called Baghdad International Airport, now eerily a ghost complex. The terminal had been stuck in a time warp since the Gulf War in 1991, when international travel to and from Iraq had been frozen. The old clicker boards still listed flights to locations like Rome and Paris, the departure times fixed to 'Delayed'.

Waiting there was an Australian lieutenant colonel, the head of a small contingent of four Australian intelligence officers working for the ISG. He welcomed me and pointed out that I wouldn't be part of his team. No, I would be working for David Kay, I said. 'Well,' he replied with a sigh, and delivered the news: my putative boss had just left for Washington, not to return. I was now a special advisor with no one to advise.

As we drove the few kilometres to the CIA base camp, I had a million questions, but mostly my mind was on what my role might now be. After passing through all the security barriers, with US guards peering at me through the SUV's window – I did not yet have all the security passes – we entered the camp, codenamed Slayer.

The colonel told me he thought the name referred to St George, the dragon slayer, but it seemed unlikely to me that the Americans would pick a UK icon to name a CIA camp.

Camp Slayer had been a former palace complex belonging to Saddam Hussein. It was roughly 1.5 kilometres by 1.5 kilometres, surrounded by a high wall and barbed-wire fencing, and contained a series of impressive buildings, a few of which had been bombed in the recent conflict. These buildings were separated by artificial lakes, and the excavated earth piled to form a sizeable hill, the sides of which were planted with various exotic species, apparently to evoke the Hanging Gardens of Babylon. A spiral road gracefully wrapped itself round the hill, connecting the top with the rest of the sprawling complex. At the summit, the US Army had built a look-out to survey the pancake-flat landscape for external threats. It all seemed surreal that this palatial complex was the main CIA base in Iraq.

However, the CIA staff and other civilians on the site lived a lot more humbly than Saddam and his prestigious guests had done. Most were housed in rows of porta-cabins replete with bunk beds, each holding about six to a room. Washing facilities were communal and basic. I could imagine life for the average CIA officer was not very comfortable.

As a special advisor, I had been given the status of brigadier-general. The lieutenant colonel showed me to my quarters – another porta-cabin, though a little more spacious than the average, with its own bathroom and, most importantly, privacy. Not the Hilton, but more than adequate for my needs.

The next morning, with no David Kay, my first port of call was the head of the British contingent. The United Kingdom had sent about twenty specialist intelligence officers to help with the weapons hunt, and this group, which included Hamish, was headed by a brigadier. I thought he might be able to explain why David Kay had left. He told me that at first Kay had been full of energy, keen to find the weapons that he so strongly believed were in Iraq, but as time went by, he gradually came to realise that he was on a wild goose chase. The weapons did not exist. In the weeks before his departure, Kay looked greatly troubled, the brigadier said. 'He was like a man who had suddenly found there was no God.'

The ISG had two components. The intelligence side was run by the CIA, and the 700-strong military contingent provided security. Despite Bush's confident 'Mission Accomplished' declaration six months earlier, Iraq was still volatile and unsafe. Every inspection team that left the CIA base camp in Baghdad was therefore accompanied by a military escort of between thirty and fifty armed soldiers, ready to shoot as necessary (and sometimes, even as not necessary). This military component was headed by Major General Keith Dayton. As he was the most senior person in the camp now that David Kay had left, I thought it would be a good idea to drop by his office.

I took an immediate liking to General Dayton. He had an intelligence background and understood the challenges of the task ahead. I came to learn that he had a sharp mind and weighed all the evidence before making decisions.

His first words to me echoed those I had heard before leaving Australia, and again on arrival in Baghdad: 'You do realise that you don't work for me?'

I did, but was beginning to wonder who I was working for. I was not working for the Australian government, nor for the absent David Kay. But I had been in similar situations before and decided to relish the free hand that had been dealt me; I could do my own thing. So when Dayton asked if I would consider guiding the ISG until a replacement for Kay could be found, I readily agreed. This was the sort of challenge I lived for. I pointed out that my contract did not allow an executive role, so I could not give directions to the CIA teams, but I was happy to advise them on what I thought they should be doing. In any case, I was aware the CIA officers might ignore direct instructions from me, since in their eyes I was an 'alien'.

That settled, Dayton alerted me that a progress report on the ISG's work was due to Congress in February 2004. I offered to write it, folding in contributions from the various sectors. Dayton expressed his gratitude, and I left his office a little unsure if I had bitten off more than I could chew.

It was now time to meet the ISG, to see what had they been doing for the past few months and what had they found or not found. Hamish was my point man for this. He had a reputation at the ISG as a guru. His intelligence background was well known, and he also had a profound knowledge of Iraq, gained through about fifty UN missions into the country. His powers of observation and eye for detail were highly respected at all levels, and although officially he was only one of the workers, his informal standing in the ISG was second only to David Kay's.

After a few coffees with Hamish in the camp's canteen, I began to understand how the ISG worked. In some ways, it was an efficient investigative unit. It was divided into specialised groups: nuclear, chemical, biological, missiles and so on, each led by a well-qualified expert. But there were a couple of problems in practice. First, many of the team members were quite junior and had no experience in their field; they were all the CIA could muster as volunteers to a war-ravaged and dangerous Iraq. To them, it was a bit of an adventure and perhaps an opportunity to advance their career. Second, the teams were almost exclusively focused on investigating the intelligence that Powell and others from the US administration had used to justify the war with Iraq. Hamish explained with a wave of a hand that everything was premised on the belief that there were hidden weapons somewhere out there, and all they had to do was find them. No one wanted to admit that the intelligence could have been wrong, and so there was no investigation of why and how it might have been wrong.

The challenge was to change the mindset in ISG. But this seemed nearly impossible, given that the CIA at Langley was almost certainly the driving force.

One thing working in favour of the investigation was that many of the senior Iraqi weapons scientists had been incarcerated in a CIA prison not far from the camp. The prisoners included Dr Taha and General Amer Rashid. I felt ambivalent about them being locked up. They had not actually committed any crime: no matter how repugnant the manufacture of biological weapons or, for that matter, any weapon of mass destruction might be, it was not illegal under international law. Indeed, the United States and the United Kingdom had done similar things at one time. On the other hand, if we were to resolve the outstanding issues over Iraq's weapons of mass destruction, these people were the key. There could be no good reason for them not to reveal the truth to us now. My hope was that this would happen quickly and they would soon be released.

Hamish told me that the prison holding these 'high-value detainees' (HVDs, as the CIA abbreviated them) was called Camp Cropper, named in commemoration of a soldier who had died in an operation the previous year. To the Americans, the slang expression 'to come a cropper' had no meaning, but to those of us with a British background, the name seemed rather odd. I was keen to visit to see the conditions there.

After many more questions about life at the CIA camp, Hamish and I left the canteen for the short walk to the CIA headquarters, where the intelligence staff were based. We had not gone far when a woman about my age ran up to me with a striking smile and embraced me like a long-lost friend. As I was endeavouring to shift her brown hair from my eyes, she exclaimed, 'Rod! Rod, I'm so pleased you're here.'

I tried to think who this was. Then it hit me: it was Laura, a CIA biological weapons analyst I knew from intelligence exchanges from my JIO and DIO days. We had a short conversation. She was now the head of the biological team hunting for those notorious 'missing' weapons. I told her I was looking forward to talking with her more.

Hamish and I continued along a canal towards an impressive building on the edge of one of the large lakes. This was the Perfume Palace, once one of Saddam's many, and now the headquarters of the CIA operation in Iraq. It was a large circular building with a domed roof, and because of its similarity to a mosque, had escaped Coalition bombing. As we entered, Hamish pointed to an Arabic inscription above the grand entrance that referred to Saddam Hussein's presence as being as sweet as perfume. Somewhat disparagingly, he pointed out that most of the CIA staff were not even aware of the inscription, or for that matter cared.

After more security checks, we climbed the stairs to the first floor, which revealed a circular open space with rooms off to the sides. In the centre was a very ornate Babylonian column, holding up the domed roof, which was about 20 metres high. The area was lit by eight elaborate chandeliers – although on closer scrutiny it was obvious they were plastic and the lights just LED. Even though the room was obviously designed to impress, with marble walls, floors and staircases, much of it looked cheap and the workmanship shoddy.

In contrast to Saddam's era, the open space was jammed with desks, cabling and computers. There was the buzz of more than 100 intelligence officers planning inspection missions, writing reports or researching intelligence leads. It reminded me a little of a beehive. As we walked around this tangled mess, Hamish pointed out one of the perimeter doors, which was painted green. It harkened back to a 1950s song, 'Green Door', with the line 'what's that secret you're keeping?' He told me he had never been through it – it led to a CIA-only room. Even US intelligence officers from other agencies were barred from entry. What went on inside, he could only speculate.

Finally, we got to my office, which had been set aside, awaiting my arrival. It was entered through one of the perimeter doors, this made from solid cedar and ornately carved. The office had 5-metre-high ceilings, from the centre of which hung another plastic chandelier. There was a conference table big enough for about a dozen people, and at a far end of the room, on a raised platform, a desk with a computer allegedly connected to the CIA network. I would soon discover that, as an alien, I was not entirely to be trusted, and the material I could access had been heavily filtered. But it was a leap forward from what Hamish and I had faced when we last worked with the CIA, at GATEWAY in Bahrain, a dozen years earlier.

Apart from the spaciousness of the room, what I liked best was a high arching window that gave a view across the flat Iraqi landscape. Hamish told me not to get too excited about having a window: the Perfume Palace was one of the tallest buildings at Camp Slayer, and was therefore the target for mortar attacks. He had heard that US Army technicians would soon come around to fit Kevlar curtains to stop shrapnel, flying glass and bullets. (In the event, my bullet-proof curtains were fitted, but I did not close them, even though on a couple of occasions I did witness shells landing close to the palace. My time in Somalia had been more hazardous than this, and I had grown accustomed to risk.)

It did not take me long to settle in. I already knew quite a few of the CIA staff from earlier encounters, and even a couple of the Brits from my time in London and at UNSCOM. The issues they were grappling with had occupied me since 1991, so I was also familiar with most of the context. What I needed to know was what the teams had found over the past five months on their sorties into the wilds of Iraq, and what the incarcerated Iraqi weapons scientists had told them. Once I had learned this, I could start putting the report together for the Congressional committees, with contributions from the teams.

I arranged individual meetings with the heads of each team. I explained what I would be doing and discussed where they were in their investigations. This went very well until I came to my meeting with the head of the chemical team, Sharlene. She was a young, clearly ambitious CIA officer who had accelerated up the ladder. Outwardly she seemed cooperative, but getting any real information from her was difficult. My questions about details usually elicited responses like, 'Well, we're still investigating that aspect.' She would then go on to explain the forthcoming missions she had planned for her team.

The meeting with Laura, who headed the biological team, was not much more enlightening. She volunteered bits of information, but further questions were answered with, 'I'm not an expert in that area, so I don't know.'

Clearly something was going on with these two. There was an undercurrent of intrigue. However, both promised to produce a draft of findings to date by mid-January 2004, and that satisfied me for the time being.

I didn't have a clear idea what sort of report US Congressional Committees might be wanting – after all, this was my first. I drew up an outline of what I thought would be acceptable and included a section at the end I labelled 'Tentative Conclusions'. While there were still unanswered questions, I thought it would be useful for us to give the committees our assessment of the miasma of information we had. We were the experts in weapons of mass destruction, and a simple data drop was probably not what they wanted. I titled the outline 'Progress Report', with the subtitle 'Findings of the ISG to February 2004'.

Apart from report writing, I was also busy attending various senior planning meetings. The focus at these was the collection of evidence to support pre-war CIA assessments, particularly those that Powell had used in his presentation to the Security Council in February 2003. While recognising that this was important, I felt that our investigations should be broader, and that we needed to get a better understanding of the Saddam regime, and how its weapons programs fit in. I had to be careful, though, because I knew that if I made any suggestion that the pre-war assessments may have been wrong, I would have been strongly opposed.

I had little success in changing the ISG's approach. For example, Sharlene's chemical team had been making repeated visits to an alleged chemical weapons storage site in the hope of finding evidence. I thought I had managed to sway the planning committee that this was futile and her team's efforts would be better spent looking at how the chemical program had been organised, what objectives it had and what had been achieved. Much to my frustration, I discovered that just a week after the committee had apparently accepted my views, her team was off again to the same site for the fifth time. This seemed a waste of resources and, given the ongoing conflict, an unnecessary risk.

General Dayton took a short break to the United States over Christmas, and on his return, I showed him my outline for the progress report. I knew, of course, that I did not work for him, but it seemed the courteous thing to do. He was grateful and suggested that since it was a CIA report, we should check with CIA headquarters at Langley whether this is what they wanted.

The next day, the two of us had a video conference with John McLaughlin, the CIA's deputy director, to see if he thought we were on the right track. He seemed pleased. When I pointed out that there would be some tentative conclusions, he seemed fine with this as long as it was made clear that things could change if significant new intelligence came to light. McLaughlin also advised that a new deadline had been agreed; the report was now not due until mid-March. This came as a relief. I expected it to be quite a substantive report.

After the video conference, Dayton surprised me with a question. 'Do you mind if I ask you something? You seem to have taken control here, and I wondered if that is just because you saw a vacuum, or is there something else?'

I was perplexed about what the 'something else' could be. I had no secret agenda and told him so. I began to wonder if someone had been whispering in his ear or he had become aware of my suggestions at the planning meetings. He noted what a strange situation it was: 'This is an American operation, a CIA operation, but you're an Australian!'

I too thought it odd, and almost certainly unique in our world of intelligence.

By the end of January 2004, the progress report was shaping up well. Working with the teams, I had put together about 150 pages, including annexes, and I was reasonably pleased with it, except for a couple of major omissions: both the chemical and biological teams had missed their deadlines for handing in their contributions. Reminders seemed to have little effect and it was becoming a battle of wills between me and the two intransigents, Laura and Sharlene.

By now I had a good idea why. When David Kay had returned to Washington, his message to anyone who would listen was that there were no hidden weapons in Iraq. The media reported his view that the work of the ISG was '85 per cent done', meaning that, while there were still some loose ends, the substantive questions had been answered. I could only agree. In fact, my progress report would reflect exactly that sentiment.

This, of course, was not a message that the Bush administration – nor, for that matter, Blair and Howard – wanted to hear. The implications were clear: the 2003 war, which had cost so many lives and brought chaos to the country, was not justified.

If anyone had doubts about the meaning of David Kay's '85 per cent done' comment, his view was clarified when he appeared before the Senate Armed Services Committee on 28 January 2004 and stated that 'we were almost all wrong' on the existence of weapons of mass destruction in Iraq. The search for the weapons had largely been completed, and it was now evident that the pre-war intelligence, almost all of it, had been faulty. The enormity of this statement and the implications for the CIA could not be overstated.

But the CIA was not simply going to wave the white flag. The leadership, particularly director George Tenet, believed that there were weapons hidden somewhere in Iraq and that, with persistence, they would eventually be found. It was evident that the ISG was now being run direct from Langley. I was beginning to be sidelined, but I still had a report to produce for Congress, and I planned to present our findings as objectively as I could. I was not going to spin the language just to satisfy the CIA; this was how the world got into this mess in the first place. Yet I could see that I was now heading for a direct confrontation with the most powerful intelligence agency in the world. I did not like my chances.

My battle with Laura and Sharlene over submitting their findings intensified. It became like spy versus spy, except we were meant to be on the same side. I suspected that both of them had personal motives. Soon I discovered that they had each made major contributions to the pre-war intelligence assessments on Iraq. My guess was that they now did not want to write anything that might contradict these assessments. Careers are made and lost on such matters, and for the young Sharlene in particular, this might be a disaster. In any case, their bosses back at Langley were telling them to continue searching, so continue they did.

By contrast, the nuclear and missile teams made much more effective use of their time. This was probably because neither team was headed by a CIA officer; the missile team was headed by a highly respected Brit and the nuclear team by a Los Alamos scientist, both of whom were fiercely independent. These teams had made timely contributions to my report and had explained how the Iraqi weapons programs had been put together and why some of the intelligence used to initiate the war was wrong.

For example, the nuclear team had debunked Powell's assertion that the aluminium tubes Iraq was importing were for enriching uranium for nuclear weapons. Iraq had indeed imported high-specification tubes, but these were for 81-millimetre-calibre rockets. On the instruction of Saddam's deputy prime minister, Abd al-Tawab Mullah Huwaysh, the Iraqi military had made rockets of this calibre, but they turned out to be very inaccurate. Huwaysh demanded that the accuracy be improved, so the military set up a seventeen-person committee to find a solution. The engineers on the committee decided that the problem was with the quality of the Iraqi-manufactured tubes: they were neither sufficiently straight nor perfectly round, and the wall thickness was uneven. They assessed that Iraq was not capable of making suitable tubes with such tight tolerances, and that the only solution was to import them.

Even after deciding on the appropriate specification, the committee thought that, just to be on the safe side, it would be wise to up the tolerances one more step. The fact that the tubes would now be far more sophisticated than needed and would cost about five times that of a lower specification did not concern the engineers. What did concern them was failure. All the members of the committee knew that in Saddam's Iraq, failure could mean imprisonment, or worse, especially when there was such high-level interest in the project. Fear was a tool the regime used to achieve results.

The nuclear team had found all this out by interviewing the members of the committee; by interviewing Huwaysh, who was incarcerated in Camp Cropper; and by analysing documentation such as the committee minutes.

How the CIA had come to this faulty conclusion was evident from what they told Colin Powell. Powell, in his presentation to the UN Security Council, had said: 'It strikes me as quite odd that these tubes are manufactured to a tolerance that far exceeds US requirements for comparable rockets.'

It was true that it was 'odd', but the CIA experts who had briefed him did not understand how Iraq worked. The CIA had assumed that if the United States would not use such tubes for rockets, neither would Iraq, and therefore the tubes could only be for uranium enrichment. Interpreting another country's actions through your own standards and culture is a basic intelligence analytical failure; at spy school it is referred to as 'mirror imaging'.

I just could not elicit anything from Sharlene and Laura, no matter how hard I tried. One morning I was looking for Sharlene, who I knew was somewhere in the Perfume Palace but nowhere I could spot. Ah, I thought, she's behind the Green Door – the door that could only be opened with a special CIA security card.

I knocked on the door and a junior CIA officer cautiously opened it and peered out. Seeing me, he ushered me in, somewhat to my surprise. I navigated around a room divider that screened the inside from prying eyes. I half-expected to find a cocktail bar and chaise longues, but instead down the centre of the room was a long bench table and a row of computers. There were codes and other information pinned to noticeboards. One whiteboard caught my eye. I only had time for a furtive glance, but almost immediately spotted my name buried alongside many others. Some names I recognised as senior ISG managers, but others I did not know. Perhaps they were CIA staff back at Langley. Perhaps they were field operatives in Baghdad. Connecting the names were arrows going this way and that, but I had no time to make sense of it. Still, it was clear that this was a little outpost of Langley, with a direct, highly secure connection back to headquarters. I had little doubt that this was where Sharlene and others got their instructions.

Sharlene spotted me and, flustered, ushered me out of the room, but I had seen enough. The ISG was supposed to be an independent body as far as its investigations were concerned, but now it was clear to me that Langley was really calling all the shots on the biggest global question surrounding Iraq.

* * *

One matter that I really wanted to find an answer to: was the information in Document X correct? It had bearing on a more central question: was my conclusion that there was missing anthrax correct?

Hamish had already discovered much of the truth. Iraq had declared to the United Nations that the production of anthrax had ceased on 31 December 1990. This had always puzzled me, because the Gulf War did not start until 17 January 1991 – surely with war coming, production would be surging until the very last moment? Iraq had also declared that all the anthrax had been destroyed in July 1991, at the Al Hakam site where it had been produced, and the inactivated anthrax dumped just outside the fence. Extensive sampling by a team led by David Kelly seemed to contradict this. So what had happened to it?

Dr Taha, now with nothing to lose and her freedom from Camp Cropper to gain, spilled the beans to her CIA interrogators. Extra anthrax had been produced, she said, as Document X indicated. But it was not destroyed at the place and time that Iraq had told us. There were fears within the Saddam regime that when the war started this valuable but dangerous biological agent would be targeted in the US bombing campaign. The bombs and warheads filled with anthrax, as well as excess bulk anthrax in containers, were therefore loaded onto semi-trailers and moved around the country, away from Hakam, for safety. Temporarily, the semis were parked at the Electronic Warfare Unit 114 (as revealed in Document X), but when the UNSCOM inspections started in April 1991, the semis were on the move again, to make them harder for the inspectors to find.

Iraq realised that sooner or later the UN inspectors might stumble across the trailers loaded with drums of anthrax. The order therefore came from Saddam, at the end of July 1991, for it all, including the extra anthrax, to be destroyed.

When the edict came through, one of the semis had broken down on a road adjacent to Radwaniyah Palace, and the whole convoy had pulled over while it was being fixed. But an order from Saddam obviously took priority, so Dr Taha's crew accompanying the semis 'deactivated' the anthrax and poured the destroyed material into the desert adjacent to the road.

The reason Dr Taha could not put this into the official Iraqi declaration or tell the Gang of Four was that a disclosure of a dump of anthrax outside one of Saddam's palaces probably meant a death sentence for her. I also wondered whether the anthrax had really been 'deactivated', as she claimed; I had my suspicions it may have just been dumped, making the risk for her even greater if she revealed this. I could now understand her tears when I came close to the truth in my questioning of her during the UNSCOM days.

Document X had proved to be correct. However, my conclusion on anthrax – featured in Blix's statement to the Security Council – that 'it might still exist' was wrong: the anthrax no longer existed.

Iraq had lied to us, but we could not possibly have guessed the reason for the lie. Now we knew the truth, and could confirm Dr Taha's story through interviews with several others.

Hamish and I visited Radwaniyah Palace, and as we stood at the foot of the steps to the entrance, Hamish pointed out the area not far from the gates where the anthrax had been dumped. Poignantly, he said, 'If only she had told us the truth. Her lies over the anthrax have cost Iraq dearly.'

I could only nod in agreement.

Laura, who likely knew of Dr Taha's confession before I did, needed my help on the anthrax question. One of the prisoners at Camp Cropper was Taha's boss, General Ahmed Murthada. I knew him quite well, and Laura, probably at Langley's insistence, thought that it would be a good idea for me to interview him at the prison to see if I could elicit any further information.

This would not be my first time at the CIA prison. I had arranged a visit sometime earlier to see the conditions there. The commandant gave me a guided tour and was forthcoming when I asked him about the details of daily life there.

The prison had been built in the Saddam era, but had been extended by the US Army. For a prison, conditions seemed reasonable. The cells were small and a bit airless but, unlike under the old regime, there was just a single prisoner to a cell. There was a good medical centre, which was frequented by the inmates, many of whom were now in their sixties. Food was basic, and meals sometimes consisted of only a US Army ration; having lived on these during my

UNSCOM inspection days, I could well understand why there were complaints. But the US Army was gradually introducing more fresh produce, as well as taking other measures to make life more tolerable.

Yet I was plagued by the question of whether many of the prisoners should even be in Camp Cropper. The ISG had most of the answers on weapons of mass destruction by now, and there seemed little purpose to their continued incarceration. Prison life takes its toll. I had spotted an elderly inmate limping around the exercise yard, some distance away. As I watched him, I came to the shocked realisation that this was General Amer Rashid, Dr Taha's husband, the man who had made threats against me a few years earlier. I had no affection for Rashid, but it was sad to see him under these conditions. I hoped he had not seen me, as I did not wish him further humiliation as he limped along in his orange jumpsuit.

Now I was back at the prison to interview another former Iraqi general. The interview room was a windowless porta-cabin furnished with a table in the centre and a few chairs. An air conditioner rattled away, trying to combat the desert heat. Hamish, who was jetlagged after taking a short break home, was with me as a notetaker. Even so, the whole interview would be secretly monitored by a hidden CCTV camera.

We sat on one side of the table, waiting for General Murthada to be escorted in. There was a little tap on the door, and Hamish opened it. Standing outside was Murthada, a US Army prison guard behind him, who ushered him in. I found this an awkward moment. On my very last UNSCOM inspection, in December 1999, just before relations between the United Nations and Iraq collapsed, I had spent a lot of time interviewing General Murthada, along with Dr Taha, about the missing bacterial growth media. Then, he was a man of influence, a minister of state, and had a certain arrogance that went with his position. He had an armed bodyguard who followed him everywhere. On my last interview with him, we both went off to the men's room during a break. At the urinal, I became aware of someone standing close behind us. It was his bodyguard, pistol drawn. I had never taken a piss under such odd circumstances. And now, here at Cropper, he had a guard of a different kind standing behind him.

I invited General Murthada to take a seat. He had lost weight since I'd last seen him, and it was clear that his former arrogance had gone. He must have felt demoralised by his current status, but nevertheless he seemed genuinely pleased to see me, a familiar face from earlier (and for him, better) times.

I interviewed Murthada for about three hours. I was particularly interested in whether he could confirm, or add to, Dr Taha's story about the convoy of semitrailers carrying anthrax around the country in 1991, and being stored for a while at Electronic Warfare Unit 114. At that time he had been the Minister for Communications. Although he said he was aware of Electronic Warfare Unit 114, he claimed he did not know about, or could not recall, the anthrax being stored there. In fact, he could not add anything further to Dr Taha's story. This did not entirely surprise me. Although on paper he was Dr Taha's boss, the biological weapons program was very much her project, and details tended to be kept within her circle.

He seemed genuinely disappointed about not proving helpful. I suspected this was because he thought if he had the information I was seeking, it might be the ticket to his release.

During a coffee break, he went outside for a cigarette, all the time being watched by the US Army guard. I joined him for an informal chat.

When out of earshot of the others, he whispered to me, 'Mr Rod, you must help me get out of here. You know my family, my daughters – they need me.'

I had never met his family, but his daughters' names were imprinted in my mind. They were called Safah and Manal – the codenames he had given to the anthrax and other biological agent production facilities, as the Gang of Four discovered during the UNSCOM inspections.

I would have liked to tell him that I would try to help, but I was aware there was nothing I could do, and I let him know that. He looked acutely dejected at this news.

When I returned to Camp Slayer, I spoke with some of the leading CIA staff to see if there was anything that could be done to free Murthada. I told them I was convinced he had nothing more to tell us. They said the message would be passed on (no doubt when they went behind the Green Door), but as I now know, Murthada spent almost another two years in Camp Cropper before his release at the end of 2005.

* * *

I knew that the CIA would not for much longer tolerate the leadership crisis the ISG had found itself in. I was not surprised when General Dayton told me that George Tenet had appointed someone to replace David Kay. He asked me whether I knew the appointee, Charles Duelfer. I actually knew Charles quite well. He was a former assistant secretary of state, dealing with security-type issues, but I knew him from UNSCOM, when he had been its deputy chairman.

Charles had a good, but rather odd, sense of humour, which appealed to me, but sometimes landed him in a bit of trouble. More importantly, he was a lateral thinker. Given his background on Iraq and weapons of mass destruction, I felt confident that although he had been appointed by Tenet, he would not be toeing the party line. I was certain, too, that he could deal with the intransigence of Laura and Sharlene. I was looking forward to his arrival in mid-February 2004, so that I could finally complete the progress report.

Charles's arrival coincided with an unannounced lightning-fast visit by George Tenet. After a ten-minute meeting with General Dayton and Charles, Tenet came out to the central hall of the Perfume Palace to address the assembled CIA staff and the hangers-on, such as Hamish and me. His 'speech' was as notable for its length as for its content. He beckoned to Charles – 'Charlie, come here,' as if he was commanding some kind of obedient dog – and wrapped a meaty arm around Charles's shoulder. I felt instantly sorry for Charles. But worse was to come. With his free hand pointing at 'Charlie', presumably so as not to cause any confusion about whom his next words were directed at, Tenet told the masses, 'This man is as weird as shit. But he knows a hell of a lot about Iraq.' A less appropriate way of introducing the new boss, I could not imagine. The look of acute embarrassment on Charles's face is still imprinted on my mind. I could see that he wanted to escape the clutches of Tenet and hide in a hole somewhere.

The next bit came directly from a football coach's manual. Almost yelling, he said, 'Iraq has hidden weapons out there and it's your job to find them!' He waved his arms around, as if to show the staff where to look. 'Are we 85 per cent done?'

The mass knew what was expected and responded reluctantly: 'No.'

Tenet repeated the cry, yelling, 'Are we 85 per cent done? I want to hear you!'

'No,' roared the CIA crowd.

And with that, Tenet turned on his heel and left, his coterie of bodyguards behind him.

This was to be my only encounter with the director of the CIA, and I was underwhelmed, to say the least. He had reinforced the message that CIA staff were clearly getting behind the Green Door, and I wondered where things would go from here. Politics was once again taking precedence over intelligence findings. I felt I was in a time warp, back in the bad old days of Yellow Rain, where facts were ignored in the name of political expediency.

I went to see Charles later that morning, to share the progress I had made with the progress report. Of course, it would now be his report, and he may want to do things differently.

Different it was. He did not even want to see my draft, dismissing it with a wave. What he wanted was a very short report – closer to twenty pages than 200 – that would focus on the work yet to do. This reflected what Tenet had told the troops. As I saw it, yes, there were loose ends to tidy, but we were well and truly more than '85 per cent done'. We knew the answers. There were no hidden weapons. I felt it was our duty to say this. Of course, it was always possible that we could stumble across some new evidence and we should include that caveat, but as professional analysts we could be reasonably confident in our conclusions.

No conclusions, Charles said, not even tentative ones. He explained that since the report was due in just over a month, he would not by then be sufficiently familiar with the issues to argue them out at the Congressional committees. Given the complexity of some of the material, I could sympathise, but I told him I would help, and if he received briefings from the team leaders, he could fill in the gaps.

Charles would not be turned. I wondered if he was under instruction from Tenet or someone else in the administration, but he denied this. Although I believed him, I thought that Tenet and probably George W. Bush must have given their views on what they expected of him in this role, and I wondered whether this had swayed him from the path of righteousness.

As his adviser and friend, I felt compelled to steer him to tell the world what we had found, or not found, and made several more attempts at changing his mind. For the most part he tolerated this, despite becoming somewhat irritated at my persistence, but still would not budge. In fact, I have since heard that he described me as 'a bit of a pain in the ass', but moderated it with, 'but you need those. They're the ones who give a crap.' After all the years of working on Iraq's weapons of mass destruction, he was right. I certainly did give something – I placed a lot of value on telling the world the results of our investigations.

I considered quitting the CIA then and there. Hamish had also had enough and told me he was preparing to leave, and there were rumblings from one or two other non-Americans who saw that the exercise had become futile. I decided to discuss the situation with the British brigadier, whose views I valued. He too was unhappy with this latest development, but argued, 'If you go, there will be no one to keep them straight. And you might still be able to influence the report.'

I could see the logic in this. I could at least try to 'keep the bastards honest'. I decided I would not leave until this new report was finished.

It took me just a day or two to draft the new report. Charles decided to change the title to 'Status Report' and I wryly thought this was a good idea: it gave the reader no expectation of any 'progress'. Under instruction from Charles, I very briefly summarised some of the activities of the ISG over the past few months, site visits and the like, and mentioned, without comment, some of the things the teams had seen. It all seemed a bit pointless. For example, to say that we had discovered that Iraq had imported some small quantities of sodium fluoride without explaining whether it was to make nerve agent or toothpaste seemed not at all helpful.

As an intelligence analyst, it was anathema to me that the report had no assessment of any kind, and no conclusions. I had many times counselled junior intelligence analysts when they had submitted a report just stating what they had uncovered without analysing its significance. Now I was doing the very same thing.

The rest of the report was on work the ISG planned to do, but even here there was no detail; it would have been impossible for the reader to determine how much further work was needed to resolve the identified issues. We might just as well have photocopied a few pages from *The Magic Pudding* and given it to Congress – at least those would have been entertaining.

Charles seemed reasonably happy with this non-report, and after a bit of tweaking told me that he would submit it to 'capitals' to see if they had any comments or suggestions. The Brits were the first to reply, with an email from John Scarlett, Sir Percy Craddock's replacement as head of the UK Joint Intelligence Committee. Scarlett's email said the report was 'light on impact'. He had picked out and suggested incorporating nine 'nuggets', as he called them – issues of concern – from a report that David Kay had written in September 2003. All of these had now been discredited, as Kay himself had made clear, so what the hell was Scarlett trying to do?

It seemed to me that he was attempting to sex up our report in the same way as The Dossier had been. It did not take me long to convince Charles we should not accept any of this nonsense.

Comments from Washington came a day or two later. The CIA also wanted some changes, one of which was to support a recent public statement by Tenet. This time Charles did not need any convincing not to include it: the proposed amendment would have raised issues that Charles did not want to get into. Most of the other changes suggested by the CIA, I could live with after some modification.

After London and Washington, Canberra's comments seemed like minor editorial matters, and so after a few further tweaks, the report was essentially finished. And so was I.

The next evening, I dropped by Charles's office to tell him I was leaving. He was surprised and somewhat upset by my imminent departure. I explained that I had not mentioned this earlier because I didn't want it to seem like a threat when I had been arguing with him over the report. It was a rather sad farewell.

I went to see General Dayton the following morning. Unlike Charles, he was not surprised by my news. He said he was sorry to see me go and, as a little memento of my time at Camp Slayer, he presented me with his personal medal as a farewell gift.

Lastly, I dropped by to say goodbye to my friend, the British brigadier, who already knew my plans. He reminded me that although the report did not say much, at least there were no lies in it: perhaps I had 'kept the bastards honest'. I reminded him that Congress had spent in the order of $500 million dollars on this exercise, and all they would get for it was a twenty-page report saying nothing. And with that, I caught a plane home to Canberra.

CHAPTER 11

THE SEARCH FOR THE TRUTH

'If you're offered a seat on a rocket ship, don't ask what seat! Just get on.'

Sheryl Sandberg, chief operating officer of Facebook

The Iraq fiasco was like no other in living memory. The 2003 Iraq War was fought for geopolitical reasons following the terrible terrorist attacks of 9/11. However, the invasion had been justified on the basis that Iraq posed a threat to world peace because of its weapons of mass destruction. We now knew that the intelligence was dead wrong.

As many as half a million Iraqi lives were lost as a direct or indirect consequence of the war, and almost 5000 Coalition soldiers were killed. Many times more than this had been injured on both sides, and in Iraq, where medical services were fairly basic, a bleak future awaited these casualties. I had witnessed firsthand the devastation to the country, not only to buildings and infrastructure, but to the political system. The country had been torn apart, with factional fighting and a breakaway group, the Kurds, that had carved out its own autonomous region in the north. Just as troubling was the rise of terrorists associated with al-Qaeda, who found Iraq's political instability a fertile ground for recruitment.

It was the politicians who made the decision to go to war, but it was the massive failure of CIA intelligence that had facilitated it. In my view, the CIA was as culpable as their political masters.

It was the end of March 2004, and it was good to be back home with Jan after so many months away. I was done with Iraq and the CIA's purported intelligence. I may have disentangled myself from the ISG, but I still had to separate myself from the Australian Defence Department. I had broken my contract with my early departure. Also, I still held Top Secret and other clearances, and I needed to go through the procedures to divorce myself of these.

My first port was my old stomping ground, the Defence Intelligence Organisation at the Russell Office complex in Canberra. As I had guessed, I was not welcomed. To senior management, I was persona non grata – not because my views on Iraq's weapons of mass destruction were diametrically opposed to those still being espoused by the Australian government under John Howard, but because I had quit my role with the CIA in protest. This was seen as damaging the relationship to an unforgivable degree.

The management declined to meet me. I suppose they did not want to be associated with my crime. I was, though, permitted to give an informal talk to some of the specialist analysts that worked on weapons of mass destruction issues, and a meeting was set up for the following week. After all my years of service in intelligence, this felt a rather ignominious departure.

Next, I visited the Defence headquarters to see Myra Rowling, the head of the International Policy Division. I knew Myra from my early days in intelligence, when we were both junior analysts. She had deservedly moved up the ranks and was now a First Assistant Secretary of Defence. She was also the person who had arranged my contract to work for the CIA and now the one who would have to sign off on terminating it.

Over coffee, I explained to Myra the reason for my resignation and handed her a letter that put it on record. She listened politely, with little comment, seeming to accept my arguments. So I was a little surprised when she thanked me for making the decision to quit. She explained that, although the CIA's official position might have become farcical, if the Department of Defence had had to pull me out, it would have upset the Americans and would have required explanations at a ministerial level. It was much better that I had made the decision myself.

This seemed a cop-out to me. I felt what she was really saying was: we are with you all the way as long as it's your neck on the block, not ours. I thought it pointless to comment. Also, I had a more important matter to raise with her.

Just before leaving Iraq, Hamish had told me that the United Kingdom had changed its policy towards prisoners at Camp Cropper. The UK government had assigned a few interrogators to work with the Americans, but had pulled them out over concerns of prisoner abuse perpetrated by US guards. We discussed this, and tried to piece together the nature of the abuse and where it occurred. During my tour of Cropper, I had seen no obvious signs of it, but of course the commandant was hardly likely to point it out to me.

We had both seen a few induction photographs, taken when the prisoners first arrived at Cropper, and several of the prisoners had obvious bruising to their faces. General Dayton had questioned the head of the interrogation unit about this, and his answer was that the prisoners had resisted arrest and had sustained the bruises then. Hamish, the good intelligence officer that he is, had done his own probing. It was difficult for him to find anything substantive, but he had heard rumours of an interrogation technique called Purgatory. After a prisoner's arrest, his head was covered in a hessian bag and he was bundled off to a unit adjacent to Cropper, where he was deprived of food and sleep for three days. During that time, his head still covered, he would be kicked and punched at random intervals and then questioned about what he knew. The theory was that prisoners are most vulnerable right after their arrest and therefore most likely to talk. This was considered valuable if the ISG was to find the 'hidden' weapons.

Although I did not have concrete evidence of prisoner abuse, the change in UK policy suggested that the Brits had seen enough. I summarised the evidence to Myra and suggested that Australia should adopt the same policy. Myra made no comment, and I assume was mulling over how to approach the issue, especially after I had already upset the CIA with my resignation.

My contract was to continue for another week so I could give the talk at DIO. A week later I was back there, presentation ready.

The director's executive assistant escorted me to the area where the analysts of weapons of mass destruction worked. I was told that there was to be no formal presentation, but I could talk to the analysts individually, as long as he was present. So now I had my own minder who was listening carefully in case I said anything that might corrupt these vulnerable intelligence officers.

But I did learn that Charles Duelfer was visiting Canberra and would be giving his own presentation in DIO that very afternoon. I asked the executive assistant if I could attend. He demurred; space was 'limited'. I pointed out that although I had left the ISG prematurely, Charles and I were on friendly terms – so could he check with senior management if 'space' could be made for my attendance? He returned a short while later and said not only could I not attend, senior management did not even want me in the building when Charles arrived. Feelings were obviously running deep. I left and, as it turned out, never set foot inside again.

I had heard that General Dayton was also in town, and was scheduled to present a medal to an Australian officer for services to intelligence. The presentation was to be in the chief of Defence's conference room in the main Defence building that very afternoon. I decided to go to the presentation, but thought the best way of getting in was perhaps not to ask for an invitation – even though I had met the chief, General Cosgrove, a couple of times. So I rolled up at the General's office, told the staff I was there for the presentation and was ushered into the adjacent conference room and greeted by General Cosgrove. Confidence is the key to opening many doors.

The medal presentation was a casual affair over drinks and canapés. General Dayton was pleased to see me, and we chatted about the ISG and how the rise in terrorist groups in Iraq was causing greater security problems for the inspection teams. I took this opportunity to confide in him that I was banned from Charles's presentation, but if Charles would like to talk to me, I would be very happy to see him before he departed the country. Dayton said he would raise it with Charles when the two of them met up later that day.

True to his word, General Dayton passed my message on to Charles, and I took a phone call that evening from his personal assistant, inviting Jan and I to dinner at a well-known Indian restaurant in Swinger Hill. We parked outside the restaurant at the appointed time, waiting for Charles, who arrived a couple of minutes later accompanied by an individual named 'Jim'. He was Charles's bodyguard, and I could see that under his jacket he was armed. Canberra is not normally as dangerous as Baghdad, but …

Jim said he would sit at another table so he could keep an eye out for any possible trouble. Whether he expected this to come from Jan or me, he did not make clear.

When we entered the restaurant, the maitre d' approached and asked, 'A table for four?'

'No,' I replied, deadpanning. 'We don't get on with this man, and he will sit at an adjacent table.'

The maitre d' looked puzzled, but did not question me. Perhaps in Canberra he was used to this sort of behaviour. Charles just smiled; we had the same warped sense of humour.

Over dinner, Charles filled me on what had happened since my departure. Knowing that I would want to hear how the presentation of the status report went, he began there. He had anticipated some aggressive questioning from Congressional committee members, he said, but it was 'an even rougher time than expected'. He seemed to regret the encounter, but stopped short of saying he wished he had used my progress report.

He had also had a rougher time with the media than expected. While we were still in Baghdad, I had arranged for him to have a couple of sessions with a media adviser. Charles had only reluctantly agreed, but from our rehearsals with the adviser, it was obvious he needed the practice. Charles was always confident he would be able to tough it out. In Washington, he was working from a very thin script and had got mauled.

Charles had now come to the realisation that a fresh approach was required with the ISG. He planned to produce a substantive report that would not only reveal what we had not found, but also explain why. It would be set against the Iraqi political context to show how the Saddam regime worked and how key decisions were made on weapons of mass destruction. This latter I had actually started shortly before Charles's arrival in Baghdad but could not find the right people to write the section, so I applauded the initiative. Charles knew some good intelligence officers with the appropriate experience that he planned to hire for this work.

As we started on dessert, Charles asked me somewhat gingerly if I might be interested in returning to the ISG. After what I had just heard, I was a little tempted, but told him that I would have to be absolutely certain the process of searching for weapons of mass destruction was objective and honest. At this stage I was not sure he had turned the ship around, so I had to politely decline. Also going through my mind was whether Tenet would allow the ship to be turned, but I did not ask this.

On the trip home with Jan, we discussed what a sorry end all this had come to. I would watch from afar for any developments, but the next morning I would finally lose my security clearances and any access I had to the inner workings of the ISG and the CIA intrigues that went along with it. I would no longer be an intelligence officer.

* * *

Just as I was becoming used to an early retirement, tending to the roses in our garden, I received an email from Charles at the end of July 2004. He asked was there any way I would reconsider my stance on re-joining the CIA team in Baghdad. He said if I still had doubts about objectivity, I could contact other team members to seek their opinion. He added that all he was asking at that stage was that I go to London, where the ISG was finalising what he called the 'Comprehensive Report', and I could decide after that whether to go on to Baghdad.

I knew that Hamish had returned to the ISG, so I thought I would ask him. He confirmed that it was now a completely different outfit; the obstructionists had left for better things. I emailed Charles to say that I was happy to go to the review, and he put the wheels in motion.

I suddenly needed to become an intelligence officer again. The deputy director of the CIA, John McLaughlin, put in a request to the Australian secretary of Defence. With lightning speed, an open-ended contract was arranged, my Top Secret clearances were reinstated, and I was given back my diplomatic passport and handed a one-way business-class ticket to London. What a difference a day makes!

A couple of weeks later, I met up with Hamish at The Grosvenor Hotel on Park Lane, where the ISG team was staying. Over the most expensive cup of coffee I have ever drunk, we discussed what lay ahead. The report had ballooned out to about 1000 pages, but only part of the section on biological weapons had been written, mainly by Hamish himself, Laura having departed the ISG. So instead of reviewing the contents, we would be writing them.

The Brits had very kindly allowed us to work from the Defence Intelligence Staff office, which was now in the Old War Office building in Whitehall. In fact, the DIS was about to move again, so the building was half-empty, which suited us perfectly. For me, it was a bit like coming full circle. As I walked around the corridors, many of the Brits recognised me, and probably walked away thinking, *Hmm, I thought that chap left some years back.*

I was pleased with what I read in the draft. This report marked a new and honest start; it should have been done months ago, but at least it was being done now.

I had three days in London, but there was much more than three days' work to be done. The target publication date for this massive tome was the end of September 2004, which gave about a month to finalise everything. Charles asked if I was willing to return to Baghdad and help coordinate the report's completion. I agreed. I knew it would be a scramble, but after so many years working on Iraqi weapons programs, I wanted to see it through to the end, whatever that might be. Two days later I was on a British Airways flight to Amman, Jordan.

At the airport I was met by a CIA officer and whisked to a secure hotel, which he informed me I was under no circumstances to leave. The next day he would pick me up at 7 am and we would go to another secure location, he said, where a plane would be waiting for the onward journey. Sure enough, I was taken to a little airfield just outside of the city, where a small chartered CIA jet was waiting on the tarmac. The plane had only one other passenger, whom I assumed was CIA, but this was not the sort of question one spy asks another.

The intrigue continued in Baghdad, where I was invited into the VIP arrivals lounge and served a bourbon and Coke. No immigration, no customs, no quarantine procedures here! Then onwards to Camp Slayer, where I was given the very same porta-cabin as five months earlier (I was already missing The Grosvenor).

This time, my cabin had sandbags on the roof to stop stray bullets from penetrating. In fact, most of the buildings at Slayer were now protected. Word had it the problem now was not targeted attacks on Slayer, but Iraqi wedding celebrations at the weekends. To mark the happy union, guests would fire their AK-47s into the air. There had been a couple of injuries and a few close misses. According to one tale, a spent bullet had penetrated the ceiling of the canteen and landed on the plate of a CIA officer. A quick wit, the officer had yelled out, 'Waiter, there's a slug on my lettuce.' The story may have been apocryphal, but there was some truth to the danger. Most Friday nights, the sky was lit up with arcs of tracer rounds. This was a city where gunfire was very much the norm.

I discovered that most of the staff who remained in Slayer were frantically writing their final contributions for the report. Some inspections continued, and the prisoners at Cropper were occasionally being interviewed, but very little new information was coming in.

I was still very disturbed by reports of possible prisoner abuse at Cropper. I had learned that the abuse was probably being perpetrated by US Special Forces, who seemed a law unto themselves. When Charles suggested I go to Cropper and interview a couple of the weapon scientists, I declined, even though Australia surprisingly still seemed to have no policy on contact with the prisoners. Had Myra put in an official complaint to the Americans or set any other wheels in motion to make Australian views known?

By the end of September, the Comprehensive Report was about as comprehensive as it could be. At over 1000 pages, with photos, diagrams and tables, I thought it was a reasonably good report given the time constraints. Most importantly, it was objective, and told things as they were. It did not make judgements about why the CIA had got it wrong prior to the war – that was for the political inquiries – but it did explain the evidence behind all our findings.

I believed that was what Congress, and for that matter London and Canberra, would want.

I returned to Canberra in mid-September wondering whether that would be the end of my involvement in the Iraq saga. I should have guessed otherwise. Barely a week after my return, Charles asked if I would go to Washington to help present the report to the Congressional committees. This was a singular opportunity for an Australian, and I agreed in a flash.

There was a slight hitch in getting to Washington urgently. Jan and I were holidaying in Adelaide, and my diplomatic passport was locked away safely in my house in Canberra. An official from the Department of Foreign Affairs suggested that if I could send him my house key by overnight express and give him the code to my home security system, he would find my passport, take it to the US Embassy and get it stamped with a special entry visa. It would be waiting for me when I returned to Canberra.

After cutting short our holiday, two days later, on Saturday, 2 October 2004, I was at CIA headquarters in Langley, Virginia. The first of the hearings was not due until the following Wednesday, but there was a lot of fine-tuning to do. I was concerned to find that the CIA staff had stuck bits into the report. This was supposed to be an ISG report, not something written by Langley to put a more favourable spin on the CIA. But the added bits were reasonably minor, and although I did not like them, I decided to let it slide.

The report was still Top Secret. Charles, quite rightly, wanted to release as much as feasible without compromising any source, so that the world would know the truth about Iraq and its weapons of mass destruction – or lack of them. We managed to sanitise the report without losing very much, and advance copies were delivered to the committees on Monday.

With the exception of Charles, who would actually be presenting the report, we could now relax a little. The US presidential elections would begin in a month's time, but Charles had deliberately chosen not to delay the report further, so he could not be accused of being a political animal. It meant there might be some fiery questions at the committee meetings, and Charles was preoccupied with preparing.

In the lull, I had a chance to discuss the ISG with some of the CIA staff. One analyst told me that my quitting in March had been a good decision because 'after that, Charlie found religion. No one could give him advice; he did his own thing.' I wasn't sure my resignation had had such a profound effect, but I did welcome the turn-around.

As I was about to leave the building on the Tuesday evening, the day before the Senate Armed Services Committee meeting, John McLaughlin came down from his office to speak to me. George Tenet had resigned as director of the CIA for 'personal reasons', but I suspected these reasons may have included the hammering he expected for his view on Iraq's weapons of mass destruction and the advice he had given Colin Powell. McLaughlin, who was now acting director, had a more balanced approach to Iraq, and I respected him for this. Of course, he should have reined in some of his analysts and more closely questioned whether the sources they had were reliable, but it is easy to make judgements after the event. After all, it had taken the ISG and more than 100 of his intelligence officers several months of on-ground work to find the truth.

I wondered what McLaughlin wanted to say. I had only met him on video conferences, and on some matters, my views had been in direct opposition to his. But when he stepped out of the elevator, his first words were, 'I really wanted to meet you and thank you for all you have done.'

I assumed from his comments that, contrary to DIO's view, Australia's relations with the CIA had not been damaged.

We had a short chat about the ISG and what we might expect from the Senate Armed Services Committee. McLaughlin told me that he would not be attending; this was a matter solely for Charles and the ISG.

The Senate hearing began at 2.30 pm on Wednesday, 6 October 2004. Senators were seated around a U-shaped table, with Charles at a small table in the centre. Behind this were rows of seats, with the first line comprising his little ISG cheer squad of the new British brigadier, an assorted group of senior CIA officials and me. The hearing room was also packed with journalists, and for about five minutes bedlam reigned as cameras rolled and flashed. Then the room was cleared of most media, and the chairman, John Warner, a leading Republican, opened the meeting.

The proceedings were not as fiery as we expected. Much of the substance of our findings had already made it to the public in one way or another, and this took some of the sting out of the questioning. Unsurprisingly though, both sides tried to drag in politics, with the Republicans, such as John McCain, finding something in our report that supported President Bush, and the Democrats, such as Hillary Clinton and Ted Kennedy, arguing that the war was unjustified based on the report's conclusions.

A major theme from the Republican senators was that the world was better off without Saddam, and surely that was a sound reason for the war. Charles neatly circumnavigated the politics, but under questioning did acknowledge that although Iraq had no weapons of mass destruction in 2003, the ISG had established that Saddam had an intent to resume weapon programs given the opportunity. Senator Kennedy seized on this and eloquently argued that the war was not fought on 'intent': President Bush had told us that Saddam actually *had* these weapons when we went to war with Iraq.

Kennedy also asked Charles whether he thought the ISG's hunt for weapons of mass destruction was a wild goose chase. Charles's response was good: 'Senator, we weren't tasked to find weapons. We were tasked to find the truth.'

I thought this precisely and succinctly summed up the true goals of the ISG. On this rationale, eventually we had succeeded in our aim. It had cost a couple of lives and a number of injuries to the ISG staff. It had also cost an incredible US$900 million. But we had found the truth.

For me, it meant the end of a long journey. After thirteen years of struggling with the enigma of the intelligence on Iraq and the spectre of nuclear, biological and chemical weapons, I could close the book and move on.

CHAPTER 12

GOING PUBLIC

'The more of your private life you put into the public domain, the smaller your private life becomes.'

Kevin McCloud, presenter of *Grand Designs*

It was not quite over. There was one matter that I could not turn away from: my suspicions of abuse of inmates just before their formal induction into the CIA prison at Camp Cropper.

In April 2004, shortly after I raised my concerns of prisoner mistreatment with Myra Rowling, the First Assistant Secretary of Defence, terrible images of US prisoner abuse at another Iraqi prison, Abu Ghraib, had reached Australian screens. I had thought this might shake the department to adopt policies to ensure no Australian had any involvement with Iraqi prisoners. But as I had found out when I returned to Baghdad later that year, nothing much seemed to have happened.

It was true that Australia had begun its own inquiry after the revelation of the Abu Ghraib prisoner abuse, and in June 2004, Robert Hill, the Minister of Defence, had stated to parliament, 'Australia did not interrogate prisoners. Australia was not involved in guarding prisoners at the Abu Ghraib prison or any other Iraqi prison.

It was only with the release of the horrific photos in late April of this year that I became aware that abuses had occurred and the extent of those abuses.'

But what about what I had told Myra in March? Had my concerns about Cropper been passed on to the Americans? Was abuse still continuing there? And what was the policy on Australians interrogating Iraqi prisoners?

Before my employment with the CIA finished in October 2004, I followed up again with the Australian Department of Defence about my concerns, and was told that a further inquiry was underway. At last, I thought, the department is taking the matter seriously. But then everything went quiet.

At the end of the year, I contacted the Deputy Secretary of Defence to see if he could tell me of any progress in the latest inquiry. He got back to me a couple of days later: the United States had been informed of my concerns about Cropper, he said, but their response was that as 'Barton had not witnessed prisoner abuse nor had direct knowledge' of it, 'the investigation could not proceed further'.

This seemed to miss the point of an investigation. I had never claimed that I had witnessed the abuse, but the evidence I had provided certainly seemed strong enough for investigators to follow up on my suspicions. It was almost as if the United States was saying: *we know you've seen the bodies in the basement, but since you didn't actually see anyone being murdered, there's nothing to look into.*

However, by this time I had further evidence of what I feared was happening at Cropper.

After leaving the ISG, Hamish and I had conducted our own little inquiry into prisoner abuse and had learned that there was a 'temporary detention facility', where the practice of Purgatory was inflicted on prisoners before their induction to Camp Cropper. The centre was said to be run by some US Special Forces group. Hamish had reminded me of a distinctive black building just across the road from Cropper: this is where he thought they operated from.

Now I had obtained an email from Admiral Jacoby, the Director of the Defense Intelligence Agency (DIA, the DIO's American counterpart), to the US Undersecretary of Defence Intelligence, and it corroborated our findings. Jacoby's email was classified SECRET NOFORN, meaning that it could not be distributed to foreign nationals, that is, non-US personnel. I received it through my US intelligence contacts shortly after it was declassified.

Jacoby referenced a report by two of his staff who worked for the ISG and had been assigned to a 'temporary detention facility' adjacent to Cropper. These staff described seeing burn marks on some of the prisoners at the facility. I later discovered that these resembled cigarette burns. They also reported bruising on prisoners and, on one occasion, witnessed a US Special Forces officer from Task Force 626 punching a prisoner. They had apparently photographed the evidence, but the TF626 officers had confiscated the photos and threatened them. They had reported all this to their senior officer at the ISG.

Significantly, the abuse reported by the DIA officers had occurred in June 2004, well after the worldwide publicity of abuse at Abu Ghraib. It made me wonder whether it was still occurring, despite US inquiries into such matters. Were the actions of TF626 sanctioned by the US administration?

The DIA report also fit precisely with what I had conveyed earlier in the year about the bruising on prisoners when they entered Camp Cropper, so I was particularly annoyed at the US comment that my concerns could not be followed up because 'Barton had not witnessed prisoner abuse nor had direct knowledge'.

~~(S//NF)~~ During the afternoon of 24 June 2004, we were notified that DIA personnel serving with TF 6-26 in Baghdad had informed their ISG seniors of the following:

- ~~(S//NF)~~ Two DIA, Directorate for Human Intelligence (DIA/DH) interrogators/debriefers assigned to support TF 6-26 (SOF) have observed:
  - Prisoners arriving at the Temporary Detention Facility in Baghdad with burn marks on their backs. Some have bruises, and some have complained of kidney pain.
  - One of the two DIA/DH interrogators/debriefers witnessed TF 6-26 officers punch a prisoner in the face to the point the individual needed medical attention. This record of treatment was not recorded by TF 6-26 personnel. In this instance, the debriefer was ordered to leave the room.
  - One DIA/DH interrogator/debriefer took pictures of the injuries and showed them to his TF 62-6 supervisor, who immediately confiscated them.

An extract from a 24 June 2004 info memo by Vice Admiral Lowell E. Jacoby, the director of the US Defense Intelligence Agency, raising concerns over prisoner abuse. Source: University of Minnesota Human Rights Library

I also wondered whether the policy on Australian involvement with prisoners at Cropper had changed. I knew that Australian Army interrogators had been assigned to the ISG, and indeed had met a couple of them, whom I had allowed to use my office at the Perfume Palace from time to time. Were these interrogators still working at Cropper, and if so, had they any evidence of prisoner abuse by the thugs from TF626?

Despite strenuous efforts to get answers to these questions from Defence, I repeatedly came up against a brick wall. Perhaps it was all too sensitive, and now, as a private citizen with no security clearances, no one from the Department was going to tell me.

In January 2005, when I was wondering if there was anything I could do other than leave prisoners to their fate at the hands of TF626, I was contacted by Liz Jackson, an ABC journalist. She hosted the television show *Four Corners*, and told me that the ABC was planning an episode on Iraq and its weapons of mass destruction, a kind of follow-up one year on. Could she interview me for some background?

Journalists are sometimes good intelligence officers too, and Liz was one of the best. We agreed to meet at my house in Canberra for an off-the-record chat. Even though I no longer worked in intelligence, there was an unwritten code that retired officers do not go public.

Liz interviewed me for about four hours, during which I told her about some of the machinations of the ISG and my concerns of prisoner abuse. She asked whether I would appear on camera. After a lifetime in the secret world of intelligence, this was not an easy decision. Even without revealing any official state secrets, there would be consequences to pay for breaking the code of silence: I would be a pariah, particularly as far as the DIO was concerned. On the other hand, I felt the issues at stake were too important. If I could possibly help some of the inmates at Cropper, my discomfort was a small price to pay.

The following week, the *Four Corners* film crew turned up at my house. As my furniture was arranged for the interview, I asked Liz who else would be appearing on the program. She looked puzzled and said, 'No one. You're it!'

I was surprised, but I was already resigned to my fate. After a gruellingly long day, the producer decided that he had enough footage. He asked for some 'atmospheric' shots of the front of the house, perhaps with me emptying the letterbox, but I did not allow it. The threats from General Amer Rashid still lingered in my mind and, although he was incarcerated in Cropper, I did not want to make it easier for his henchmen to carry them out – even if this was unlikely. An even greater risk to my privacy might be the media. So the producer took some silly footage of me pruning the roses at the back of the house. I felt grateful the program was not *Gardening Australia*.

The *Four Corners* episode 'Secrets and Lies' aired on 15 February 2005. It had an immediate impact. Labor politicians on a Senate estimates committee raised the issue of prisoner abuse in parliament the very next day. Unfortunately, the whole debate circled around the difference between interrogation and interview, while the broader matter of whether prisoners had actually been abused and whether it was continuing – let alone what action might be taken to stop it – was ignored.

On 17 February, the matter was again raised in parliament. Appropriately, it was the member for Barton who asked Prime Minister Howard if he was aware of what Rod Barton had said on the ABC. Follow-up questions by Labor politicians Kim Beazley and Kevin Rudd did not advance the issue of prisoner abuse because, again, the focus was on interview versus interrogation. What they were trying to do was nail the Minister of Defence for his statement to parliament the previous year that 'Australia did not interrogate prisoners'. It was all politics.

The Senate, which had a Labor majority, called for a parliamentary inquiry. The terms of reference covered most of the important matters that I had raised on *Four Corners*, so I hoped that this might have a more productive outcome.

I should have known better. I was the only witness to appear before the inquiry, in what was a new low for any parliamentary inquiry. Why no one from DIO or the military who had served with the ISG, or even Myra Rowling, to whom I had told the story of abuse, did not come forward to testify, I could only speculate. In fact, I was later approached by a couple of servicemen who said they would have liked to testify but were told by their commanding officers that they were not to; their views would be presented by a senior officer who would appear before the inquiry on the ISG's behalf. This never happened.

WITNESSES

A page from Hansard showing the entire list of witnesses to the Senate inquiry 'Duties of Australian personnel in Iraq', Senate Standing Committee on Foreign Affairs, Defence and Trade, 29 March 2005.

The debate at the parliamentary inquiry sank into political harangues. After a day of testimony and questions, nothing had been resolved. The final report concluded that in the circumstances of Camp Cropper, the meanings of the terms 'interview' and 'interrogation' had merged. I could only imagine the great rejoicing from the prisoners in Cropper on hearing this news. Apart from that, the committee decided that since I was the only witness, it could not draw any conclusions regarding the other terms of reference. The fact that no one else had testified had served the bureaucracy and the government well. Politics had again won the day.

After the parliamentary inquiry, it seemed at least that the United States started to take my concerns about prisoner abuse at Camp Cropper more seriously. I do not know what went on behind the scenes, but a few months after the inquiry, I received a call from a senior foreign affairs official, asking if I would agree to be interviewed about prisoner abuse by a US investigator. I was only too happy to oblige.

Two weeks later, the Naval Criminal Investigative Service turned up at my home. After showing me his badge, the investigator introduced himself as Supervisory Special Agent Bruce W. I was surprised that he was not accompanied by an Australian official. If an Australian special agent had wanted to interview a US citizen in their home country, he or she would have been accompanied by at least three FBI agents, and probably the CIA as well.

Bruce and I spoke for about an hour. I told him what I had seen and some of what Hamish and I had deduced but lacked firm evidence for. Before he left, I asked whether he thought he would get very far with his investigation, given that US Special Forces were involved. He seemed confident that no one could hide from the NCIS, citing an investigation he had been involved in at a US base in Okinawa where a perpetrator from Special Forces had been brought to justice.

Just over a month later, Bruce came calling again, still unaccompanied. This time, he was less confident. He told me that he could not obtain from the ISG the name of any CIA official who had been involved with prisoners at Camp Cropper. I gave him a short list of some senior people to try.

He asked, 'Do you know whether the interview reports of prisoners at Camp Cropper have been destroyed?'

I said that these were official records so should not have been destroyed. In any case, the reports would have been sent to CIA headquarters at Langley; they should have copies available for him to peruse. He explained, somewhat obliquely, that he had been told all copies had been destroyed.

I despaired, then, that the US Special Forces involved with the practice of Purgatory were above the law. Their actions had official sanction, and Bruce's investigation was going nowhere.

Even to this day, it is difficult to know what really happened at Cropper, and what Purgatory involved or who was responsible for it. But there is one Iraqi who has since spoken out, at some risk to himself. His name is General Hossam Amin – a former engineer I knew well from my UN inspection days. Amin was released by the CIA on 23 December 2005, after almost three years of incarceration, on the condition that he sign a statement preventing him from speaking publicly about his arrest or experiences at Cropper.

Amin gives a harrowing account of Purgatory. With a black bag over his head, he was interrogated for five days about Iraq's 'missing' weapons of mass destruction. During this time, he was punched, kicked and sometimes hit with a metal stick, never seeing his assailant or knowing when, or where, the next blow would come. He was told he would be executed, and he believed it: every day he told himself, *Now I will die*. At night, there was no respite: 'Even when you are sleeping, they beat you. You wake by punching.'

As traumatic as his time in Purgatory was, he said he met others in Cropper who had had it even worse. The practice was widespread, and it seems that just about all the prisoners who finished up at Cropper had been through some version of Purgatory. Even to this day, it appears that none of the perpetrators were made accountable for their crimes.

* * *

A day or two after the broadcast of the *Four Corners* episode, Jan and I were awoken by a knock on the door. A quick look at the security camera showed a reporter clutching a microphone, a film crew beside him. They had somehow managed to track me down.

I was certainly not going to open the door to this mob. It was the worst kind of journalism, if it could be called that – more spectacle than substance.

For the next few days, we had journalists show up trying to get a soundbite or brief clip. Little did they realise that our house backed onto a nature reserve, and Jan and I could quietly slip out the back and walk down the fire trail to the next street, where we had parked our cars in anticipation of this harassment. These journalists were no match for two former intelligence officers.

Everyone has their fifteen minutes. The media lost interest, for the most part. However, I was sometimes called on as a commentator after that. I was selective on what media outlets I would engage with and what issues I would talk about. The ABC and SBS usually got a nod, if the subject matter was kept to prisoner abuse or weapons of mass destruction. I always declined to get into discussions of purely political issues or the workings of intelligence agencies. Once an intelligence officer, always an intelligence officer.

One of the many stints I did with the ABC was on the Canberra ABC Radio breakfast program. I was a guest commentator on the morning news, which had an item about North Korean nuclear weapons. At the end of the session, as was the tradition, the host asked me to select a song to play. I chose 'Hotel California' by the Eagles. As I explained on-air, when I was in Bahrain with GATEWAY, the only Western music I could find in the local markets that wasn't absolutely horrendous was an Eagles cassette. I would play this constantly as I drove round the country.

Hotel California has the lines: '*You can check out any time you like, / But you can never leave.*'

This sentiment reflected, a little, how I felt about my involvement with Iraq and its invisible weapons of mass destruction. Every time I thought I had 'checked out', I was dragged back in, often as a willing participant, but not always. And so it has continued over the years, even to this day.

AFTERWORD

Throughout my career as an intelligence officer, I was required to collate information from various sources, analyse it for authenticity and meaning, and write an assessment of what I made of it and the implications for policymakers. It is the nature of intelligence that there are no absolutes: there will always be uncertainties. But on some issues, such as Yellow Rain and the alleged weapons of mass destruction that led to the 2003 Iraq War, the evidence pointed overwhelmingly away from the case made by politicians. So why did they turn a blind eye?

Politicians might argue that there are broader considerations and objectives to take into account: the facts and the truth might need to be subverted for a greater good. But this logic is flawed – one need only look to the present-day turmoil in Iraq and the Middle East for evidence of this. One thing my intelligence career has taught me is that, with a few exceptions, politicians only take professional advice when it supports their policies, and even then, only pick the bits that suit them. Current policy on climate change, nuclear weapons and, to an extent, even the coronavirus pandemic, still seems to turn on self-interest and some vague notion of the 'greater good'. I am at a loss on how to solve this conundrum.

* * *

Although I have officially left the intelligence world, I have not entirely cut the strings. In one sense I never can, because of the high-level security clearances I once had; due to the agreements I signed, I am bound by the *Commonwealth Crimes Act on Official Secrets* till death. But I have more tangible ties with the intelligence world. I keep in touch with a few of my former intelligence colleagues. I am sometimes called by entities, including the United Nations, seeking my views on a wide range of nefarious international activities. All of this involves drawing on the intelligence experience I have gained over the years.

It is largely through my intelligence links that I have followed, as far as possible, the fate of some of the scientists and engineers who once worked on Iraq's weapons programs. I believe all now have been released from Camp Cropper, most after serving two to three years, but some languished much longer than that. General Amer Rashid was only released in 2012, after nine years in prison.

What happened to all these scientists and engineers after their release becomes a bit murky. For their own safety, the CIA would fly them to Amman, Lebanon, give them $100 and ensure they signed agreements to prevent them from talking publicly. There was an implied threat that the consequences of not honouring this would be severe. Then they were on their own. A few may have stashed money away in foreign bank accounts to make comfortable lives for themselves elsewhere, but most would have had to look for jobs or financial assistance, usually in one of the Gulf States.

There is no evidence to suggest that any of these top scientists were lured by offers from other countries, such as Syria, to help them with their weapons programs. Nor do I believe that ISIS co-opted them for its chemical weapons manufacture, although it is possible that some junior scientists or technicians may have been caught up with such work. I have been reliably informed that Dr Rihab Taha was in Sana'a, in Yemen, where she landed a job at the university teaching biology. However, with the start of the civil war in Yemen in 2015, she and her daughter may have fled to places unknown. I do not know whether she ever met up again with her husband, General Rashid.

The country they left behind, Iraq, has continued in turmoil, and I see little prospect of any real peace for many years to come. The intelligence failures over Iraq cost the country dearly and bestowed a bleak future. The other country I worked in, Somalia, has not fared better. The rise of the terrorist group Al-Shabaab, a spin-off from some of the militia groups that I was trying to disarm, has made Somalia one of the most dangerous countries on Earth. All I can say about my role, both in Iraq and in Somalia, is that I did what I could.

* * *

My life took a new turn after the publicity died away. Jan's son started a wine retail business, and Jan and I joined him in it. This reignited my interest in wine, which had started when I hosted wine tastings in Henry VIII's cellar all those years ago in London.

Surprisingly, my weapons inspection work has turned out to be relevant in the wine business. Once, Jan and I visited a winery in Echuca, on the Murray River. With great enthusiasm, the French winemaker showed us the large fermenters, explaining the innovations he had made since his arrival. I saw that there was a problem with the set-up of some of his fermenters. For a moment he looked nonplussed, and then, recognising a fellow expert, said, 'Yes, I know. I tell the engineers this is not right. I tell them, they need to fix, but they do nothing.' I refrained from telling him that the fermentation of grapes to produce wine is little different to the fermentation of bacterial growth media to produce anthrax.

My intelligence career spanned over thirty years, and it took many twists and turns impossible to envisage when I started. Looking back, I cannot imagine having worked in any other job.

The 'Hotel California' syndrome sometimes manifests in surprising ways. Over the years, the DIO asked me to give a couple of talks to staff – off site, in the main conference room of the Department of Foreign Affairs. Management has not quite forgiven me: feelings at the top still run deep, probably reinforced by my *Four Corners* appearance. It has been made clear to me that I will not be allowed to step inside their building again. I've even heard rumours that staff have been instructed not to have contact with me socially. I can only guess at the machinations inside the organisation, but these occasions have driven home to me the degree of importance Australia places on the relationship with the United States. If agents have to be sacrificed, so be it, seems to be the thinking.

* * *

At St Philip's Christian College, when I finished my talk on being a spy, a fifteen-year-old girl approached me. After scrutinising me for a moment or two, she cocked her head, narrowed her eyes and said, 'You don't look like a spy.'

I replied, 'Thank you. That is the best thing you could have said.'

No spy ever wants to look like one. Perhaps she would have preferred a James Bond lookalike with a licence to kill, but maybe, just maybe, she realised that the life of an ordinary intelligence officer can be almost as interesting.

ACKNOWLEDGEMENTS

I am grateful to all those throughout my career who gave me support and encouragement, especially when times were difficult or bleak. There are too many to mention here, but they know who they are. I also thank the myriad individuals who appear in *The Life of a Spy*, whether they were opponents or allies: without them, there would have been no book!

I acknowledge publisher Chris Feik for having faith in me and agreeing to publish this book. Chris helped cast my previous publication, *The Weapons Detective*, into shape, and it was a pleasure to work with him again. There are many others at Black Inc. I am indebted to; in particular, associate publisher Julia Carlomagno. She had the patience and skill to transform *The Life of a Spy* into a more dynamic read. Thank you, Julia.

Particular thanks go to Michael Bronner for documenting the torture Hossam Amin suffered at the hands of US special forces. We need people like Bronner to expose injustices and violations of human rights if we are ever to make the world a better place.

www.ingramcontent.com/pod-product-compliance
Ingram Content Group UK Ltd.
Pitfield, Milton Keynes, MK11 3LW, UK
UKHW021840270726
14058UKWH00002B/253

9 781760 642778